Your Training Notebook On

Pop Music Special Chord Progressions

Suitable for guitar and
more musical instruments

Scott Su

Translated by
Lynda Huang

TABLE OF CONTENT

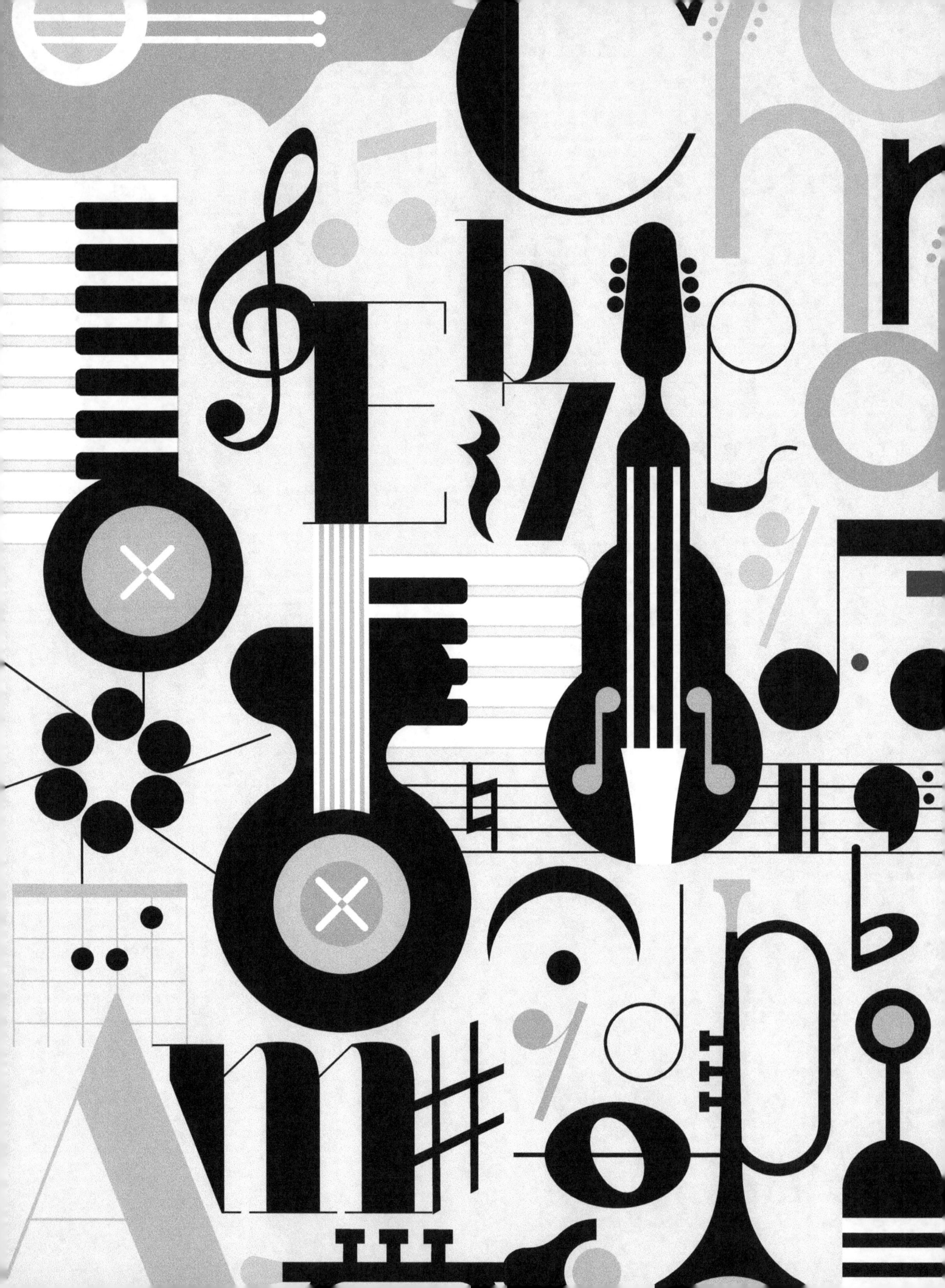

Author

AUTHOR

Scott Su, an independent music composer, producer and guitarist from Taiwan. He is also a richly-experienced studio musician, skillful in music arrangements and releases mainly guitar performance albums. His self-composed albums include "Are You Still There？", a guitar performance single and "No Flowers On Island." Scott also writes useful guitar method books which include "Fretboard Secret Handbook" , "Playing Guitar So Easy" and etc.

＊ Site：http://ScottSu.net/

＊ Facebook：http://www.facebook.com/scottmusic

＊ Album：Please search "Scott Su" on iTunes, Spotify

「Are You Still There ？」

A new acoustic guitar performance single

Compose / Arrangement / Performance / Recording / Mixing / Production by Scott Su

Harmonica by Otis Tsao

「No Flowers On Island」

Electric / Acoustic guitar performance album on iTunes

Compose / Arrangement / Performance / Recording / Mixing / Production by Scott Su

INTRODUCTION

The use of harmony and chord progression can usually affect atmospheres which a song communicates; therefore, to further understand feelings produced by different chord progressions is very helpful to your playing as well as compositions.

As pop music available in a current market are mostly written in a certain mode of chord progression, it is quite uneasy for listeners to identify different characteristics. And with quite a smaller ear range, general song composers and instrumental players, can easily be limited in a smaller frame.

Of such concerns, I therefore search pop songs domestically and internationally with more characteristics in chord progressions as references. I have listened and organized all chords on my own. In addition to listing out music with a guitar chord notation method, an analysis on harmony is also available. I hope readers who love music performing, song arranging as well as composing are able to expand depths and longitudes in music on themselves through the understanding of chord progressions. Also I look forward to more diversities in pop music of the future. The provided QR Code is for you to listen to and feel related music on Youtube.

It may possibly contain advanced music theory in relation to areas of harmonic analysis sections and more Intros are available in Chapter of Analysis and Integrations.

If readers feel it is more difficult to understand theory sections, then it is all right to omit them. As long as readers can rehearse chord progressions continuously, allowing your body to remember these different feelings, these chord progressions will naturally become a part of your music data collections. And during performances and compositions, you will naturally feel the ability to be able to choose different chords.

Certainly you can use chord progressions to practice improvisation or compositions directly. Many music masters have ever revealed that if you want your body to remember the feeling of choosing chords naturally, you will need to use them directly upon performances and composition. The last chapter is to guide you to rearrange chord progressions in a song by using harmonic approaches, and this also allows you think about how to produce different tastes or feelings when playing a song.

For readers who are familiar with the guitar, the fingerings are listed out under every chord and I hope you are able to do transposition trainings on your own upon practice times. For transpositions on the guitar, please place the root of a tonic chord to keys of different strings for practices (eg: in C key, the most often played fingering is C root chord on the 5th string. You can use the same song and transpose it to G key to practice.).

I sincerely wish you a big progress in music learning!

Scott

Chapter of Direct Trainings

To directly listen and play songs that contain characteristic chords is a very good way to learn. First, it enhances the feelings of your ears and body for characterized sections and chords, knowing how to press these chords then this will slowly become a routine habit of yours. In the end, you will be able to play these chords naturally just like playing the often use chords.

Remember to repeatedly experience and feel chord sections which you are not familiar with, and even when you are not playing them, the musical notes in chord progressions can still appear in your mind. This way is definitely easier for you to comprehend and memorize when learning methods as well as harmonic analysis in later time.

＊For the convenience of enabling key transition exercises on the chord progression of each song, this book is written slightly different from other books on chord analysis. Sections on slash chord is still notated with a forward slash (/) to represent upper voice and bass, instead of directly remarking chord series. the regular marks of a secondary dominant chord (eg : Ⅴ/Ⅱ) is not used to distinguish from a slash chord : additional explanations on a secondary dominant chord are in word analysis behind repertories.

Example I
Sample chord reference song :

Beautiful

Christina Aguilera

Form Progression

Intro → Verse → Chorus → Inter → Verse → Chorus → Verse

→ Chorus → Intro

Chord Progression

Intro

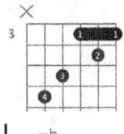	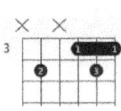	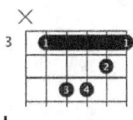	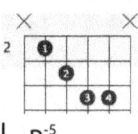	
E♭	E♭/D♭	Cm	B⁻⁵	

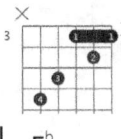	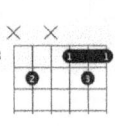	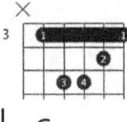	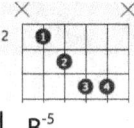	
E♭	E♭/D♭	Cm	B⁻⁵	

Verse

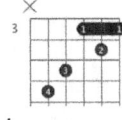	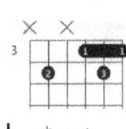	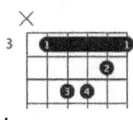	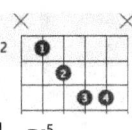	
E♭	E♭/D♭	Cm	B⁻⁵	

| E♭ | E♭/D♭ | 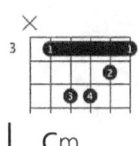 Cm | B⁻⁵ | |

011

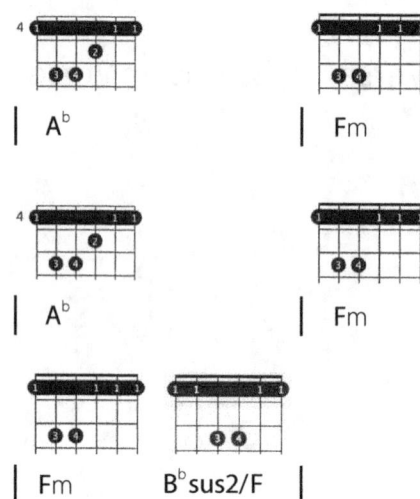

| Aᵇ | Fm | Eᵇ | Eᵇ/Dᵇ | Cm | |

| Aᵇ | Fm | Eᵇ | Eᵇ/Dᵇ | Cm | |

| Fm | Bᵇsus2/F |

Inter

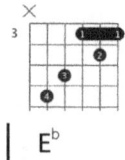 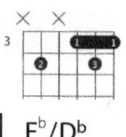 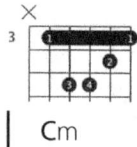 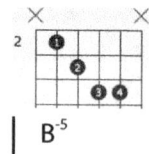

| Eᵇ | Eᵇ/Dᵇ | Cm | B⁻⁵ | |

Analysis

If you have no interests in music theory analysis or you feel theory usually just causes you nothing but headaches, then you can simply and continuously play chord progressions of this song and then pay special attention to the marked sections. Allowing your ears and body to remember the special feelings produced by chord progressions of the section. By doing so, you will be able to expand atmospheres and inspirations upon your playing, song-composing and even improvisations.

 KEY

E♭ Major Key

 CHORD SERIES

Presentation of chord is replaced as harmonic series :

Intro

	I		(FT 1)

| I | | I / ♭7 | VI m | ♭VI⁻⁵ | |

| I | | I / ♭7 | VI m | ♭VI⁻⁵ | |

Verse

| I | | I / ♭7 | VI m | ♭VI⁻⁵ | |

| I | | I / ♭7 | VI m | ♭VI⁻⁵ | |

Chorus

| IV | | II m | I   I / ♭7 | VI m | |

| IV | | II m | I   I / ♭7 | VI m | |

(FT 3)
| II m   V sus2 / **2** |

Inter

| I | | I / ♭7 | VI m | ♭VI⁻⁵ | |

① . The musical form of this song is very simple; however, even a simple chord progression uses a harmonic approach to express feelings of this song.

Here the slash chord appears in the 2nd measure of Intro, $I /^b7$, belongs to the 3rd inversion form of I 7. I 7 is not the seventh chord of I series within the key; instead, it uses I series of a parallel Mixolydian with a modal interchange technique. An inversion form allows bass voice to play musical notes outside the key for a more different musical atmospheres.

② $^bVI^{-5}$ in the 4th measure of Intro uses VI chord of a parallel minor key with a modal interchange technique.

③ . The slash chord V sus2 / 2 in the 9th measure of Chorus is the 2nd inversion form of V sus2.

How can I identify an inversion chord ?

Inversion chords are frankly quite common in applications; however, in order to identify them correctly, it takes a long period of time in experiences and practices of ear trainings. In pop music, the easiest way to identify an inversion chord is that when you discover you can identify notes upon a progression in the bass part, and in the same time, the chords sound like they are still within the same key but you don't feel right about the remaining chord notes when you use a root position to fit on them. This often then, is very possible to be a chord inversion of another series.

Example Ⅱ
Sample chord reference song：

Somewhere
Over the Rainbow

Connie Talbot

Form Progression

Intro → Verse → Verse → Chorus → Verse → Chorus End

Chord Progression

Intro

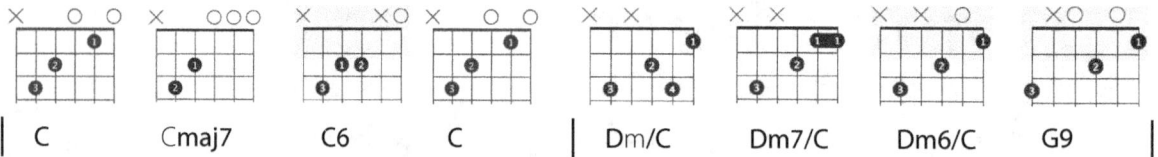

| C | Cmaj7 | C6 | C | Dm/C | Dm7/C | Dm6/C | G9 |

Verse

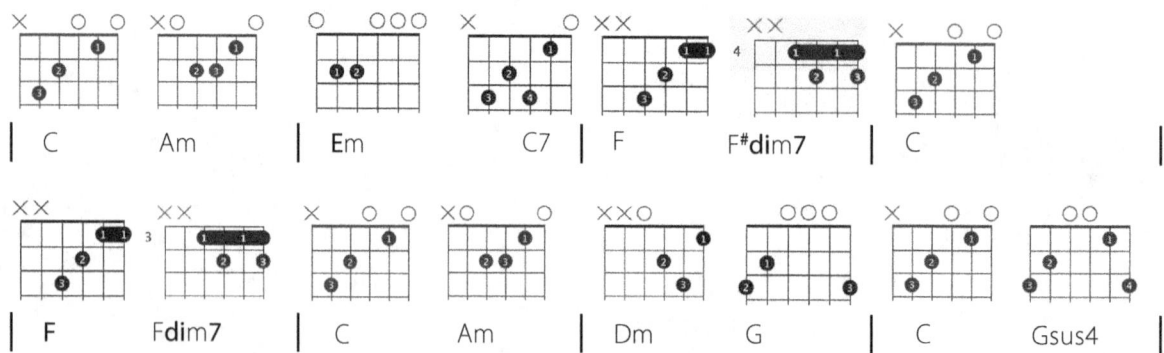

| C | Am | Em | C7 | F | F#dim7 | C |

| F | Fdim7 | C | Am | Dm | G | C | Gsus4 |

Chorus

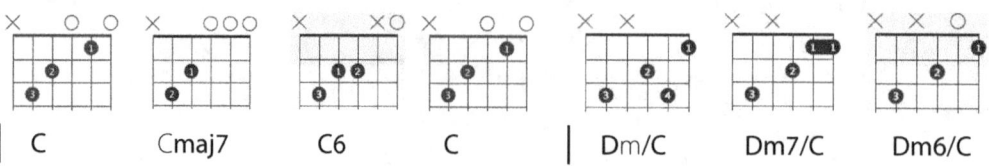

| C | Cmaj7 | C6 | C | Dm/C | Dm7/C | Dm6/C |

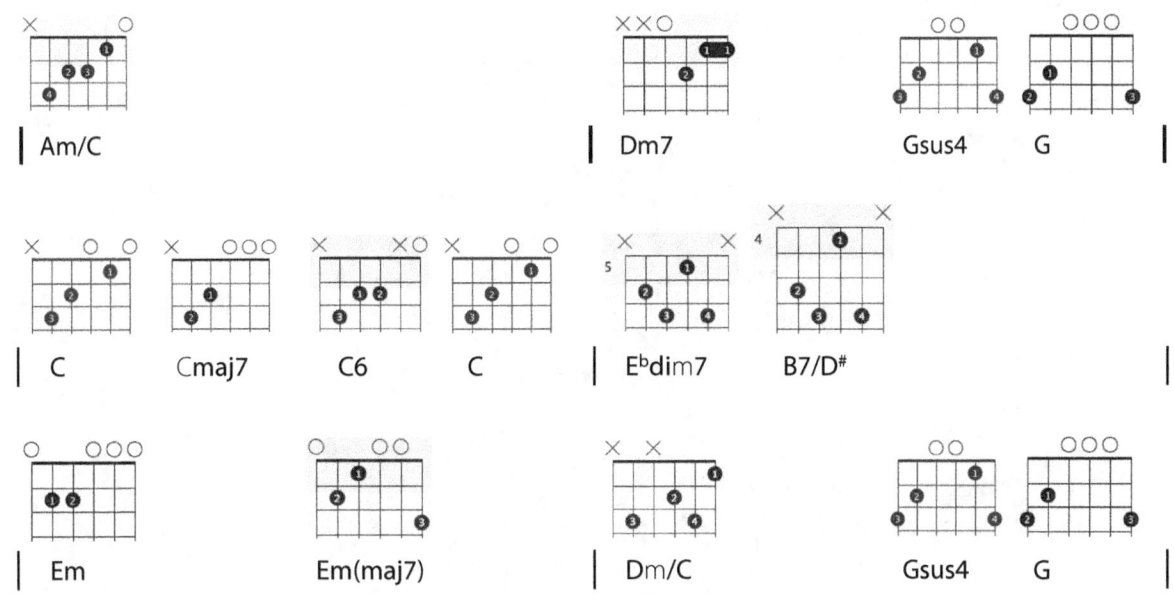

Am/C	Dm7	Gsus4 G
C Cmaj7 C6 C	Ebdim7 B7/D#	
Em Em(maj7)	Dm/C	Gsus4 G

Chorus End

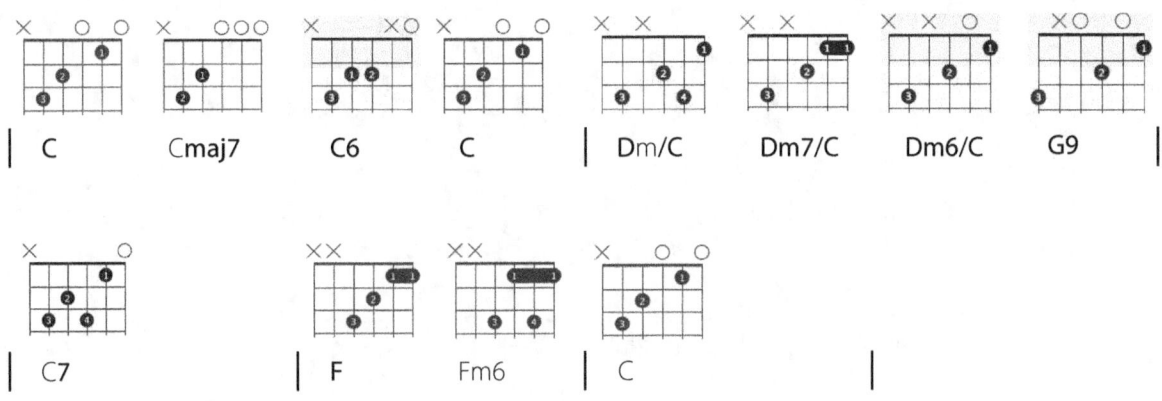

| C Cmaj7 C6 C | Dm/C Dm7/C Dm6/C G9 |
| C7 | F Fm6 | C | |

Analysis

KEY

C Major

CHORD SERIES

To present in chord series :

Intro

(FT 1)

| I | maj7 | 6 | | II m /1   II m7 /1   II m6 /1   V 9 |

Verse

                                            (FT 2)   (FT 3)

| I   VI m | III m   7 | IV   #IV dim7 | I |

    (FT 4)

| IV   IV dim7 | I   VI m | II m   V | I   V sus4 |

Chorus

| I | maj7 | 6 | | II m /1   II m7 /1   II m6 /1 |

| VI m /1 | II m7   V sus4   V |

| I | I maj7 | I 6 | I | ^(FT 5) ^bIII dim7 ^(FT 6) VII 7 /[#]2 | |

| III m | ^(FT 7) III m(maj7) | II m /1 | V sus4 V | |

Chorus End

| I | I maj7 | I 6 | I | II m /1 II m7 /1 II m6 /1 V 9 | |

| I 7 | IV ^(FT 8) IV m6 | I | |

REMARKS

① . In the entire two measures of Intro, bass voice section has been progressed in a form of tonic sustained note until the very last chord in the 2nd measure.

A single voice diatonic descending is used in upper chord for achieving slight changes in harmony.

② . I 7 in the 2nd measure of Verse is a secondary dominant chord which belongs to a V series seventh chord of the IV in the back section, progressing in V → I area.

③. $^{\#}$IV dim7 in the 3d measure of Verse is a diminished seventh chord being used as a bridge. By analyzing its previous and later composing notes, you can discover voices progressing in a chromatic approach.

④. IV dim7 in the 5th measure of Verse is a diminished seventh chord being used as a bridge. By analyzing its previous and later composing notes, you can discover voices progressing in a chromatic approach.

⑤. ^{b}III dim7 in the 6th measure of Chorus is also a diminished seventh chord being used as a bridge. By analyzing its previous and later comprising notes, you can also discover voices progressing in a chromatic approach.

⑥. The slash chord VII7 / $^{\#}$2 in the 6th measure of Chorus is the 1st inversion of VII7, and the following chord, III m, is a V → I relation; therefore, this chord is also a secondary dominant chord. By adopting an inversion form allows an effect of chromatic approach between bass voice section and the following bass chord.

⑦. Ⅲm(maj7) in the 7th measure of Chorus has formed a Line Cliché single voice chromatic approach descending mode with the previous and later chords.

⑧. Ⅳm6 in the 4th measure of Chorus End is a newly obtained chord with a parallel minor key modal interchange.

Example Ⅲ
Sample chord reference song：

She

Charles Aznavour

Form Progression

Intro → Verse 1 → Verse 2 → Chorus → Verse 3

Chord Progression

Intro

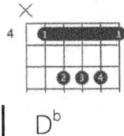 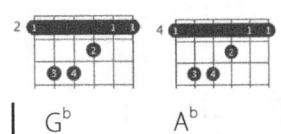

| D♭ | | G♭ | A♭ | |

Verse 1

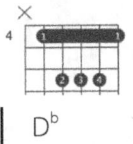 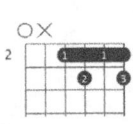 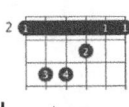 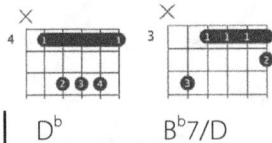

| D♭ | | F♭ᵒ7 | | G♭ | | D♭ | B♭7/D | |

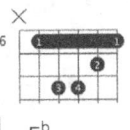 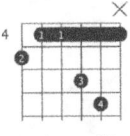 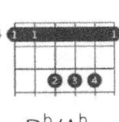 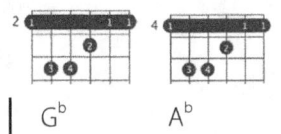

| E♭m | | G♭m/B♭♭ | | D♭/A♭ | | G♭ | A♭ | |

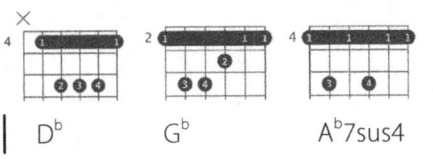

| D♭ | G♭ | A♭7sus4 | |

Verse 2

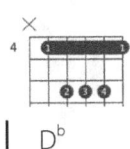 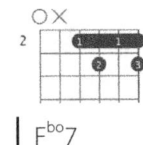 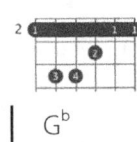 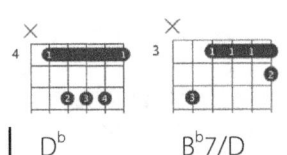

| D♭ | | F♭ᵒ7 | | G♭ | | D♭ | B♭7/D | |

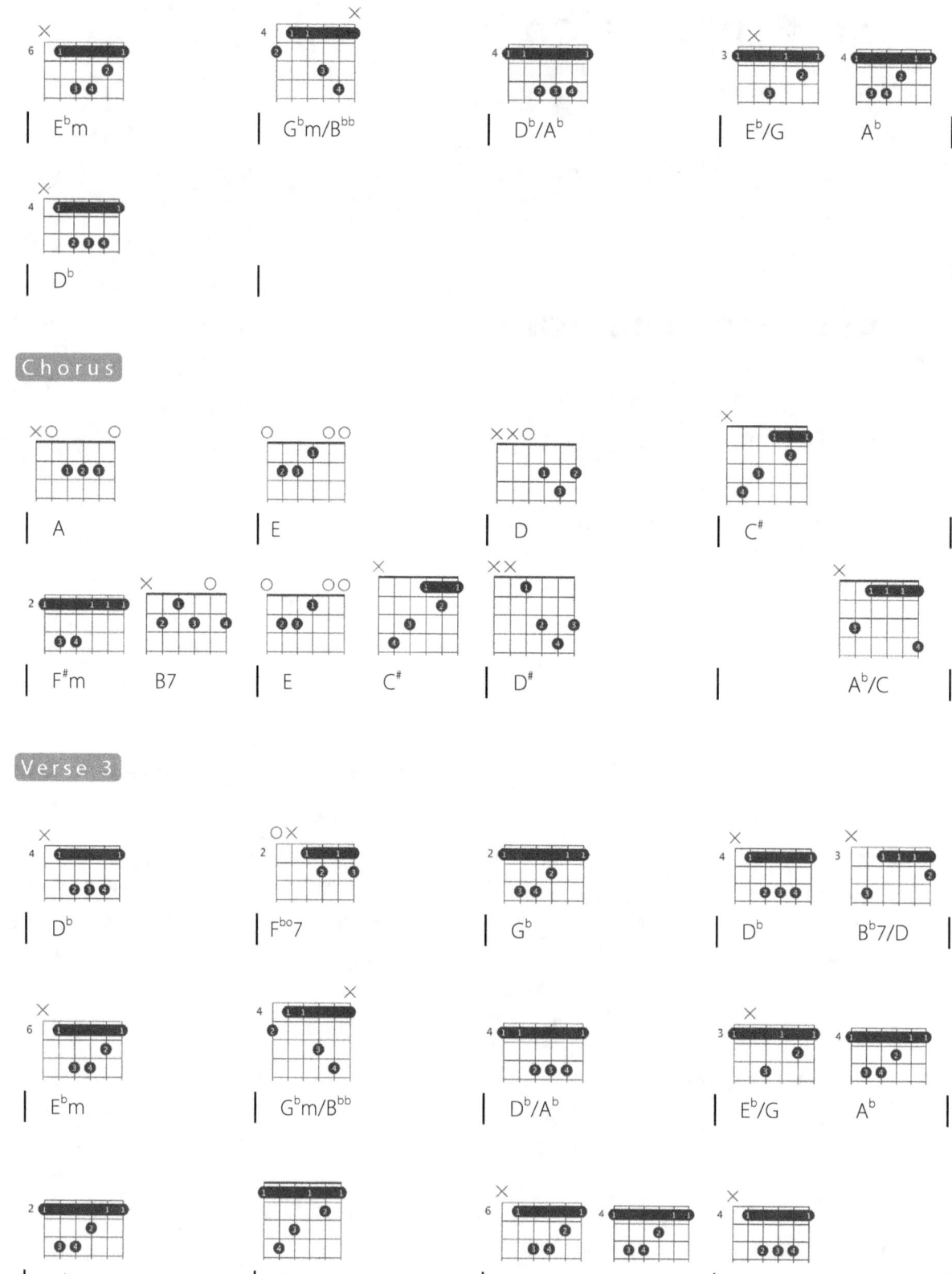

E♭m   G♭m/B♭♭   D♭/A♭   E♭/G   A♭

D♭

Chorus

A   E   D   C♯

F♯m   B7   E   C♯   D♯   A♭/C

Verse 3

D♭   F♭o7   G♭   D♭   B♭7/D

E♭m   G♭m/B♭♭   D♭/A♭   E♭/G   A♭

G♭   D♭/F   E♭m   A♭   D♭

Analysis

KEY

This song belongs to D♭ key and modulates to A key four measures before Chorus. And it modulates to an E key in the 5th and 6th measures, to a G♯ key in a C♯ chord and modulates back to D♭ key from A♭/C.

CHORD SERIES

To present in chord series :

Intro

| I | IV   V |

Verse 1

                                     (FT 1)   (FT 2)

| I | ♭III °7 | IV   IV / 6 | I   VI 7 / ♯1 |

                                     (FT 3)

| II m | IV m / ♭6 | I / 5 | IV   V |

| I   IV   V 7sus4 |

Verse 2

| I | ♭III °7 | IV | I   VI 7 / ♯1 |

                                                                            (FT 4)

| II m | IV m / ♭6 | I / 5 | II / ♯4   V |

| I |

Chorus (FT 5)

A Key							
I		V		IV		III	

E Key				G# Key				D Key	
II m	V 7	I	IV	V			V /7	

Verse 3

I		♭III °7		IV		I	VI 7 /#1
II m		IV m /♭6		I /5		II /#4	V
IV		I /3		II m	V	I	

REMARKS

①. ♭III°7 appears in the 2nd measure of Verse is a diminished seventh chord.

A diminished seventh chord is characterized by its unstable and ambiguous feelings; therefore, the chord can nearly be resolved to any other chords and not to be too sudden. Also, it is very suitable to be used as a bridge or a connecting chord for key modulation. However, in practical uses, the chord is also rich in colors of sad and miserable feelings, therefore, more considerations for the whole scenarios are therefore needed upon use.

②. VI/$^{\#}$1 in the 4th measure of Verse is the 1st inversion of VI. VI is not one of the diatonic scales in the key: the use here is that it is a connecting chord of the next Vseries of IIm for establishing a similar V-Iharmonic progression. The use of inversion allows a special chromatic approach of a 1 - $^{\#}$1 – 2 progression in the bass voice.

③. IVm/^{b}6 in the 6th measure of Verse is IV series 1st inversion of major and minor keys after a modal interchange. This inversion allows a 3rd note（^{b}6 on a scale）to be located in the bass voice, allowing the notes which are not in the original key to appear in the bass. And this gives more obvious characteristics.

④. II /$^{\#}$4 in the 8th measure of Verse 2 has an exact use as the previous VI/$^{\#}$1. It then establishes a similar V - I chord progression with the following chords. By using inversions, the bass voices have a special chromatic approach of $^{\#}$IV - V progression; and with an addition of the previous chords in bass voices, the voices then become a scale chromatic progression of a ^{b}6 - 5 - $^{\#}$4 – 5.

⑤. Modulation sections in Chorus. The C$^{\#}$（III of A key）chord in the 4th measure has an exact V - I harmonic relation to F$^{\#}$m（II m of E key）in the back, and also uses this relation to make key modulation to be more fluent. F$^{\#}$m is also the common chord of the two keys. The I chord（E）of E key in the 6th measure is seen as ^{b}VI, a minor key modal interchange chord of G$^{\#}$ key and it is used as a common connecting chord for key modulation. V（D$^{\#}$）of G$^{\#}$ key and V（A^{b}）which is modulated to the original D^{b} key in the end also has a V - I harmonic relation. D$^{\#}$ serves as the common chord for modulating back to the original key.

Example Ⅳ
Sample chord reference song :

I Just Can't Stop Loving You

Michael Jackson

Form Progression

Intro → Verse → Verse → Chorus 1 → Intro → Verse

→ Chorus 2 → Bridge → Chorus 1 (to raise one semitone)

Chord Progression

Intro

| 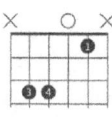 C | | | Csus4 | |

Verse

| C | | Gm | | |

| C | | Gm | | |

| F | | Fm(maj7) | Am | |

| B♭9 | | E♭maj7 | G7sus4 | |

Chorus 1

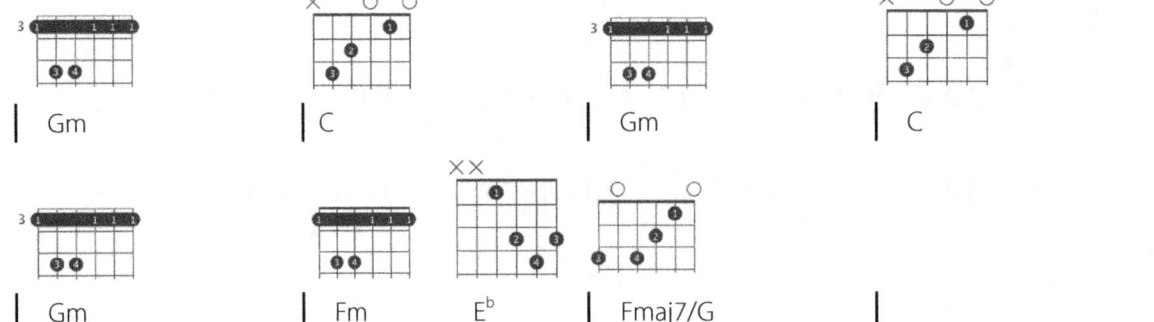

| Gm | C | Gm | C | |
| Gm | Fm   E♭ | Fmaj7/G | | |

Chorus 2

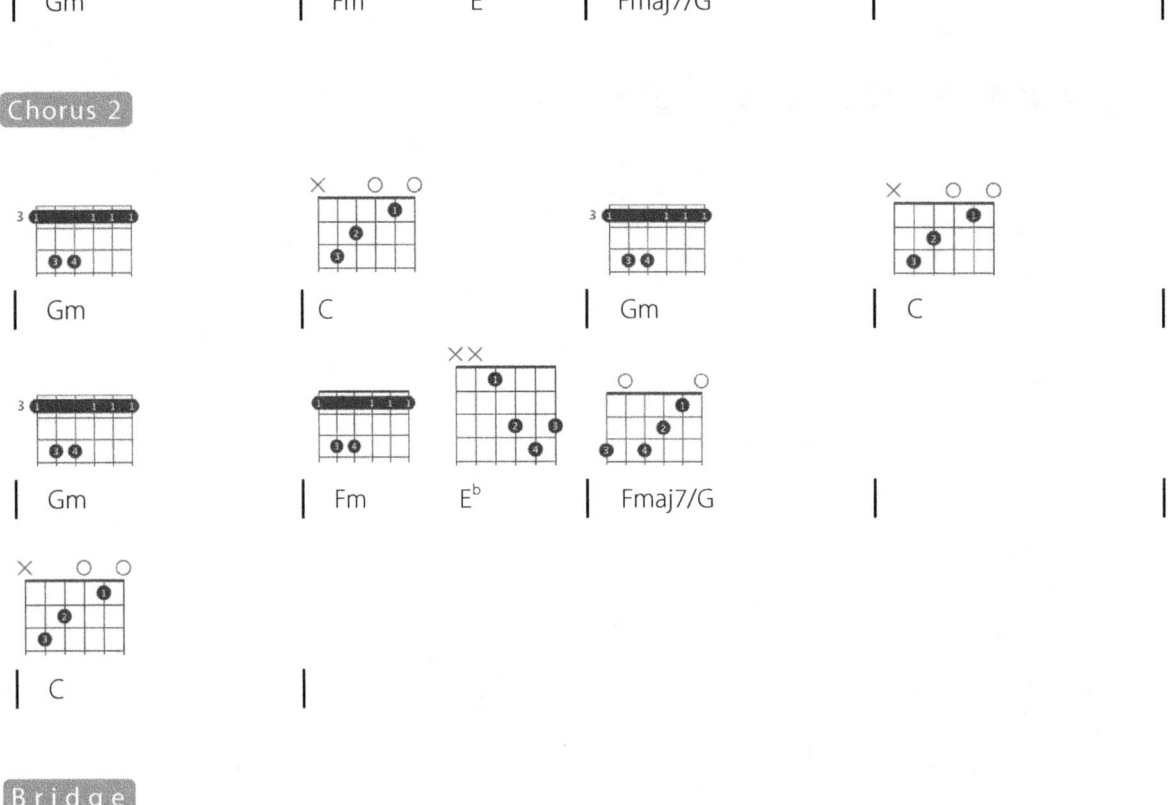

Gm	C	Gm	C	
Gm	Fm E♭	Fmaj7/G		
C	

Bridge

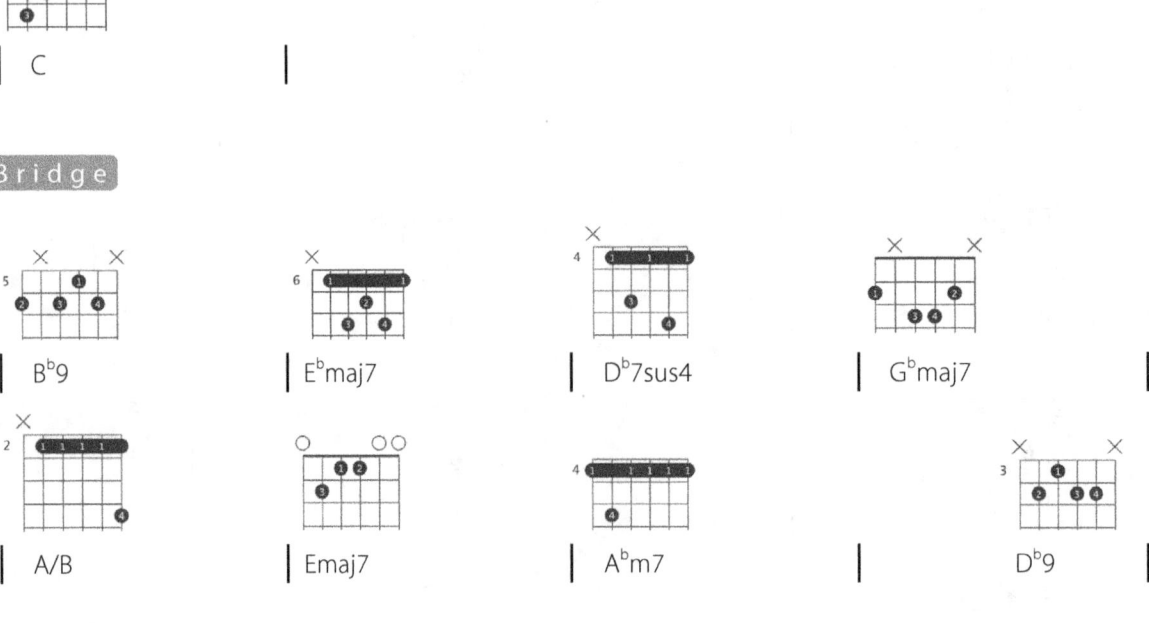

| B♭9 | E♭maj7 | D♭7sus4 | G♭maj7 | |
| A/B | Emaj7 | A♭m7 | D♭9 | |

Analysis

KEY

It starts with a C Major and modulates to E^b key in the 13th measure in Verse, and then it is back to C key in the 16th measure.

The 6th measure in Chorus modulates to E^b key and it is back to C key in the 7th measure.

As of the bridge section, it is E^b key in the 1st and 2nd measures and it modulates to G^b key in the 3rd and 4th measures. And then it modulates to E key in the 5th and 6th measures. After modulating to G^b key in the 7th measure, the last section of Chorus is a half key sharper than the original one.

CHORD SERIES

To present in chord series：

Intro

			I					sus4		

Verse 1

                                                          （FT 1）

	I				V m				

	I				V m				

                                                          （FT 2）

	IV				IV m(maj7)		VI m		

E^b Key（FT 3）   **C Key**

	V 9				I maj7		V 7sus4		

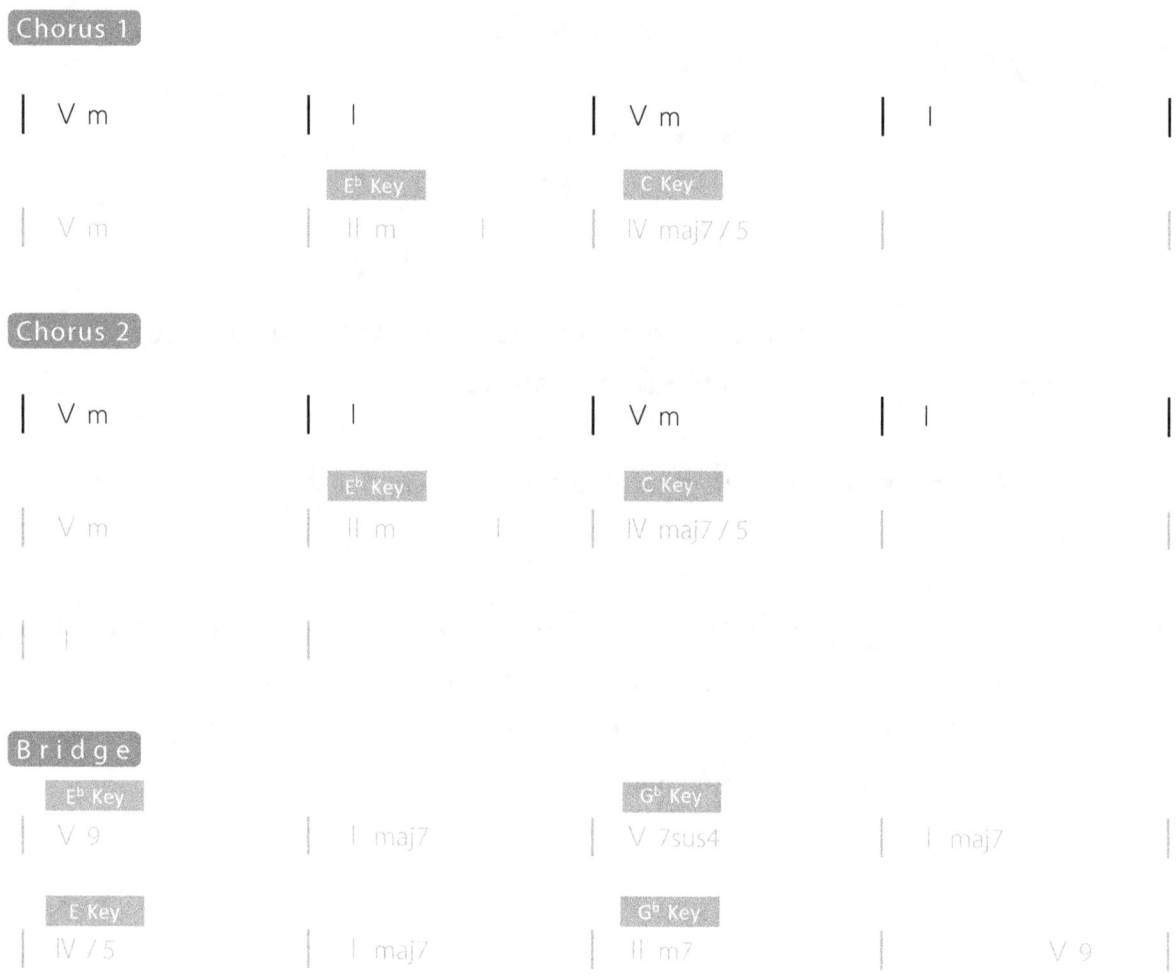

Chorus 1

| Ⅴm | | Ⅰ | | Ⅴm | | Ⅰ | | |

Eᵇ Key C Key

| Ⅴm | | Ⅱm | Ⅰ | Ⅳmaj7 / 5 | | | |

Chorus 2

| Ⅴm | | Ⅰ | | Ⅴm | | Ⅰ | | |

Eᵇ Key C Key

| Ⅴm | | Ⅱm | Ⅰ | Ⅳmaj7 / 5 | | | |

| Ⅰ | | |

Bridge

Eᵇ Key Gᵇ Key

| Ⅴ9 | | Ⅰmaj7 | Ⅴ7sus4 | | Ⅰmaj7 | |

E Key Gᵇ Key

| Ⅳ / 5 | | Ⅰmaj7 | Ⅱm7 | | Ⅴ9 | |

REMARKS

①. Ⅴm in Verse uses a modal interchange approach, to replace the original Ⅴ with Ⅴm of Ⅴ series chord in a C Mixolydian.

②. Ⅳm(maj7) in the 11th measure of Verse adopts Ⅳm of Ⅳ series chord in C minor with a modal interchange approach, and also it uses the 7th note of Ⅳm with a maj7 approach. This is so because it is the 3rd note in C major key that allows an emphasis on a major key feeling.

. B♭9 is the chord being used in the 13th measure of Verse after modulating to E♭ key. In addition to being a Ⅴ9 of E♭ key, to see this from the original key, meanwhile, it is also a ninth chord ♭Ⅶ9 of Ⅶ series in a C minor key modal interchange. We use this as a common chord for a key modulation.

♪♪ Connection of Modulation

In this song, many times of modulation are being used and designed in quite a beautiful way. And mostly, the way of doing a modulation is to use common chords used by previous and later keys（the key chords）as connections of key. Please pay special attention to that the common chord is not necessarily a chord in an ascending diatonic chord. In here, many cases that use chords generated after a modal interchange approach as a connection of common chord progression and this is like the analysis described above.

Modulations which are used in other areas are as the followings：

* In the 15th measure of Verse, E♭maj7 in C key is a Ⅲ series major third chord of a modal interchange which can be used as a common chord.

* The 6th measure of Chorus uses a common chord characteristic of E♭ key chord of which it can modulate interchangeably with C key, especially the Gm is also seen as a common chord which starts in the previous measure.

* In the 3rd measure of Bridge, the common chord 'D♭7sus4' in E♭ key is a modal interchange form of Ⅶ series in E♭ minor key.

* In the 5th measure of Bridge, the common chord 'A/B' in G♭ key is a modal interchange form of Ⅳ series extended chord in G♭ minor key.

* The 7th measure of Bridge, the common 'A♭m7（G#m7）' in E key belongs to Ⅲ series, which is also a modal interchange form of Ⅴ series in D♭ key.

Key modulation sections which are not explained are all repeated as the above descriptions.

Example V
Sample chord reference song :

Say Yes

CHAGE & ASKA

Form Progression

Intro → Verse 1 → Verse 2 → Chorus → Chorus End 1

→ Inter 1 → Verse 1 → Verse 2 → Chorus → Chorus End 2

→ Inter 2 → Chorus → Chorus End 3

Chord Progression

Intro

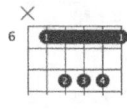

E♭		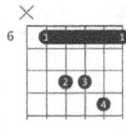	
		E♭sus4	

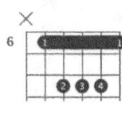

E♭		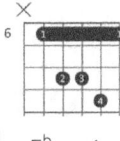	
		E♭sus4	

Verse 1

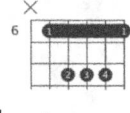

| E♭ | Fm | Gm | A♭ | |

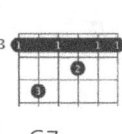 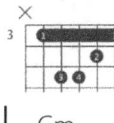

| G7 | Cm | Fm | B♭7 | |

037

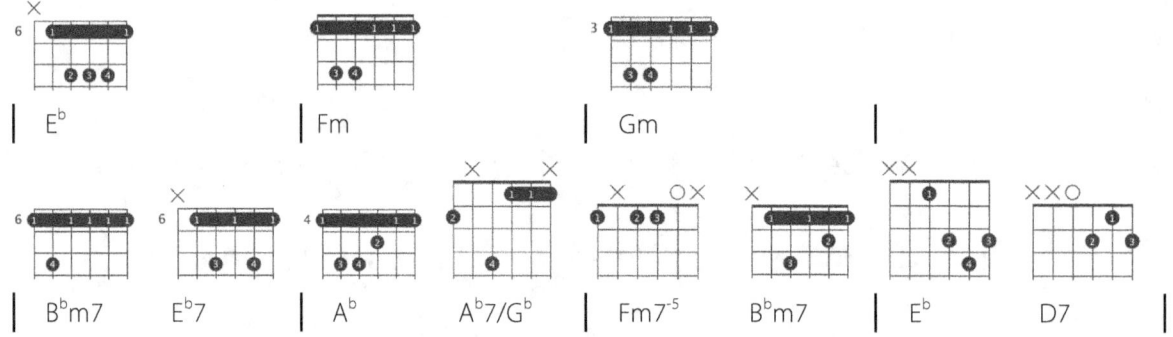

E♭ Fm Gm

B♭m7 E♭7 A♭ A♭7/G♭ Fm7⁻⁵ B♭m7 E♭ D7

Verse 2

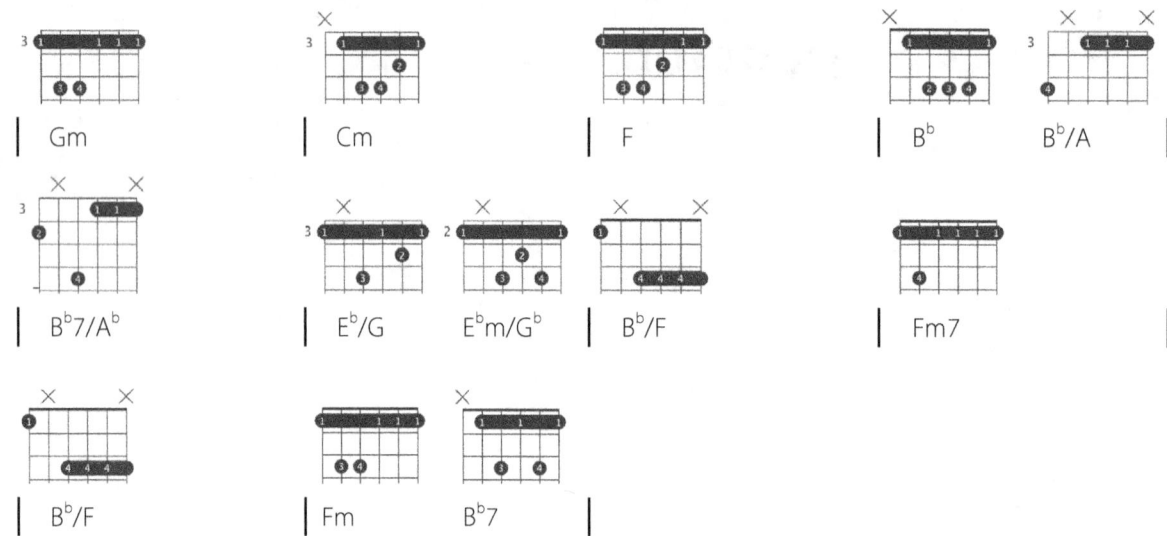

Gm Cm F B♭ B♭/A

B♭7/A♭ E♭/G E♭m/G♭ B♭/F Fm7

B♭/F Fm B♭7

Chorus

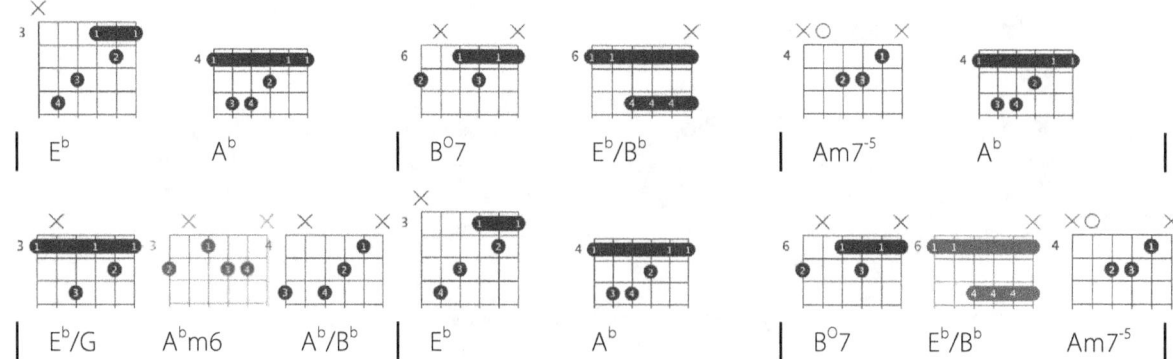

E♭ A♭ B°7 E♭/B♭ Am7⁻⁵ A♭

E♭/G A♭m6 A♭/B♭ E♭ A♭ B°7 E♭/B♭ Am7⁻⁵

Chorus End 1

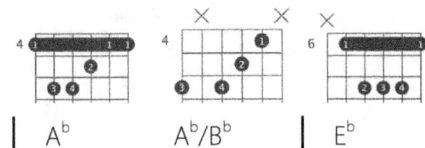

| A♭ | A♭/B♭ | E♭ | | |

Inter 1

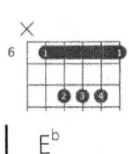 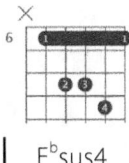 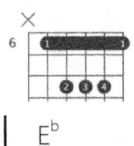 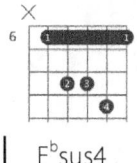

| E♭ | E♭sus4 | E♭ | E♭sus4 | |

Chorus End 2

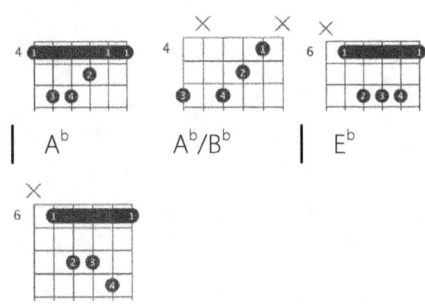 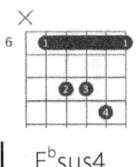 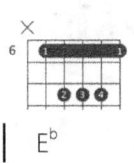

| A♭ | A♭/B♭ | E♭ | E♭sus4 | E♭ | |

| E♭sus4 | |

Inter 2

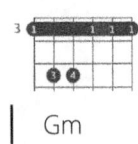 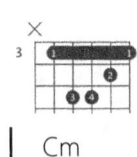 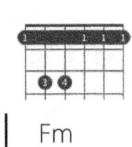 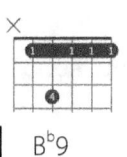

| Gm | Cm | Fm | B♭9 | |

| | |

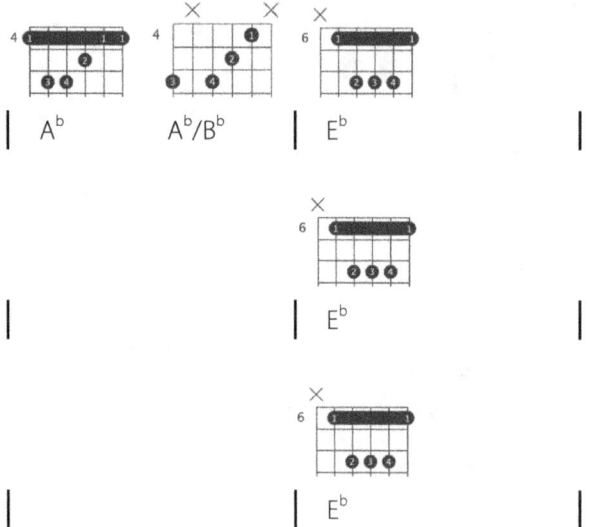

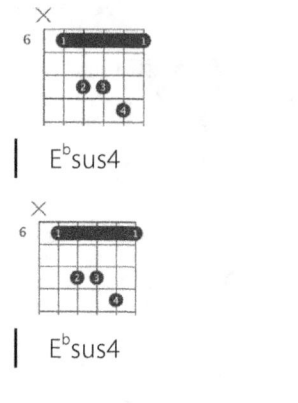

Analysis

 **KEY**

E^b key. There is a slight modulation in the 11th measure of Verse 1 to A^b key and then quickly modulates to E^b key.

CHORD SERIES

To present in chord series :

Intro

| | | | | sus4 | | |

| | | | | sus4 | | |

Verse 1

| I | II m | III m | IV | |

(FT 1)
| III 7 | VI m   II m | V 7 | |

| I | II m | III m | |

A♭ Key (FT 2)   E♭ Key (FT 3)   (FT 4)
| II m7   V 7   I | 7/♭7   II m7⁻⁵   V m7   I   VII 7 | |

Verse 2

(FT 5)   (FT 7)
| III m | VI m | II | V   V/#4 | |

(FT 6)
| V 7/4 | I/3   I m/♭3 | V/2 | II m7 | |

| V/2 | II m   V 7 | |

Chorus

(FT 8)
| I   IV | #V °7   I/5 | #IV m7⁻⁵   IV | |

(FT 9)
| I/3   IV m6   IV/5 | I   IV | #V °7   I/5   #IV m7⁻⁵ | |

Chorus End 1

| IV   IV/5 | I | | |

Inter 1

| I | I sus4 | I | I sus4 | |

IV	IV / 5	I		I sus4		I		

I sus4		

Inter 2

III m		VI m		IIm		V 9		

Chorus End 3

IV	IV / 5	I				I sus4		

		I				I sus4		

		I			

REMARKS

①. III 7 in the 5th measure of Verse 1 is a V series seventh chord of
VIm in the back.

②. B♭m in the 11th measure of Verse 1 is a V m of a parallel minor
key with a modal interchange approach in the original E♭ key. And
when it is in A♭ key, it becomes a II m. By using this chord as a
common chord for a modulation connection, we may also see this
as a progression of 2-5-1 section.

③. The occurrence of $\mathrm{II}\,m7^{-5}$ ($\mathrm{F}m7^{-5}$) and $\mathrm{V}\,m$ in the 12th measure of Verse 1 is due to a use of II series and V series of a parallel minor key with a modal interchange. $\mathrm{F}m7^{-5}$ in $\mathrm{A}^\flat$ key is formed due to VI chord of a parallel $\mathrm{A}^\flat$ Dorian with a modal interchange approach, therefore, this is used as a connection chord for modulating back to the original key.

④. The chord of the 4th beat, $\mathrm{VII}7$, in the 12th measure of Verse 1 is $\mathrm{V}7$ chord of the following $\mathrm{III}\,m$.

⑤. II in the 3rd measure of Verse 2 is a use of II series of a parallel Lydian key chord with a modal interchange approach. It is also V of a following V chord which forms a 2-5-1 progression from the previous and later chords.

⑥. Of the 6th measure in Verse 2, when I is connected to $\mathrm{I}\,m$, I series chord of parallel minor is used and both of them use 1st inversion form to allows the 3rd note in the bass voice. And this then leads to the bass voice progressing in a chromatic approach.

⑦. The more obvious descending chromatic approach of bass voice starts from V in the 4th measure of Verse 2, and this continues to move to $\mathrm{V}/2$ with a chromatic descending approach. When the bass voice uses this type of progression, chord wise, inversion chords are usually adopted to perform a matching state.

⑧. $^\#\mathrm{V}^\circ 7$ in the 2rd measure of Chorus is a diminished seventh chord and similarly from here, bass voice uses a descending chromatic approach to $\mathrm{I}/3$. In the middle of section, in addition to using a diminished seventh chord and an inversion chord as a connection, a $^\#\mathrm{IV}m7^{-5}$ uses IV chord of a parallel Lydian with a modal interchange approach.

⑨. $\mathrm{IV}m6$ in the 4th measure of Chorus is also a modal interchange of IV series of a parallel minor key.

Example VI
Sample chord reference song :

Evergreen

Barbara Streisand

Form Progression

Intro → Verse 1 → Verse 2 → Chorus → Verse 3 → Verse 4

Chord Progression

Intro

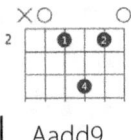 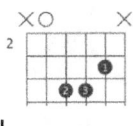 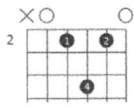 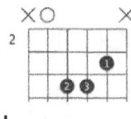

| Aadd9 | Bm/A | Aadd9 | Bm/A |

Verse 1

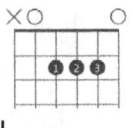 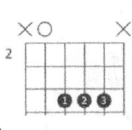 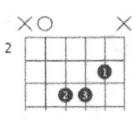 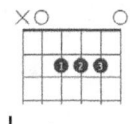

| A | B/A | Bm/A | A |

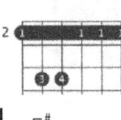 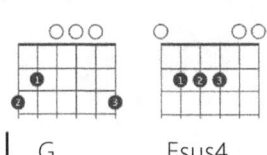

| F#m | C#m | Bm | G   Esus4 |

Verse 2

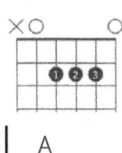 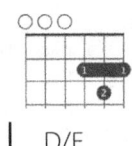 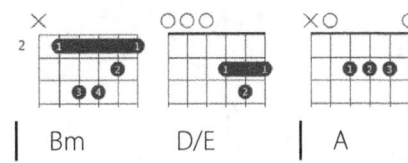

| A | D/E | Bm   D/E | A |

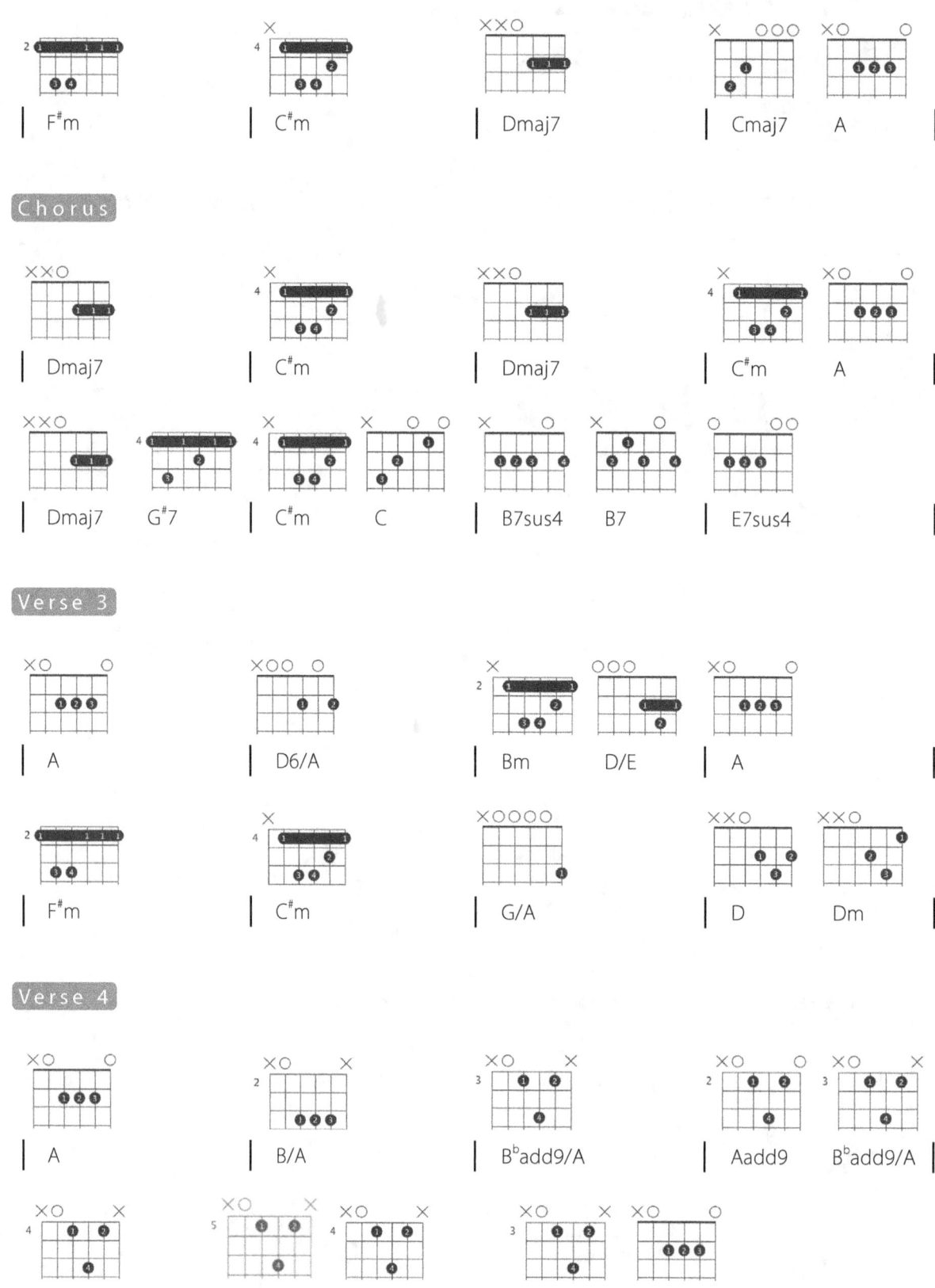

F#m   C#m   Dmaj7   Cmaj7   A

Chorus

Dmaj7   C#m   Dmaj7   C#m   A

Dmaj7   G#7   C#m   C   B7sus4   B7   E7sus4

Verse 3

A   D6/A   Bm   D/E   A

F#m   C#m   G/A   D   Dm

Verse 4

A   B/A   Bbadd9/A   Aadd9   Bbadd9/A

Badd9/A   Am11   Badd9/A   Bbadd9/A   A

Analysis

KEY

A Key。

CHORD SERIES

To present in chord series：

Intro

| I add9 | II m / 1 | I add9 | II m / 1 | |

Verse 1

| | （FT 1） | | | |
| I | II / 1 | II m / 1 | I | |

| | | | （FT 2） | |
| VI m | III m | II m | ♭ VII   V sus4 | |

Verse 2

| | （FT 3） | | | |
| I | IV / 5 | II m   IV / 5 | I | |

| | | | （FT 4） | |
| VI m | III m | IV maj7 | ♭ III maj7   I | |

Chorus

| IV maj7 | III m | IV maj7 | III m   I | |

| （FT 5） | （FT 6） | （FT 7） | | |
| IV maj7   VII 7 | III m   ♭ III | II 7sus4   II 7 | V 7sus4 | |

| I | | IV 6 / 1 | II m | IV / 5 | I | |

| VI m | III m | (FT 8) ᵇVII / 1 | IV | (FT 9) IV m |

| I | | II / 1 | (FT 10) ᵇII add9 / 1 | (FT 12) I add9 ᵇII add9 / 1 |

| (FT 11) II add9 / 1 | I m11 | II add9 / 1 | ᵇII add9 / 1 | I | |

REMARKS

① . II/1 in the 2nd measure of Verse 1 adopts a parallel Lydian to conduct a use of modal interchange; therefore, II/1 will not be treated as a chord inversion, it is however handled as an extension or a mixed chord by using '1' as root. The continuous four measures of sustained bass notes in the bass section allow the musical atmospheres be more different.

② . ᵇVII in the 8th measure of Verse 1 is from VII series chord of a parallel minor key, and this is a use of modal interchange.

③ . IV/5 in the 2nd measure of Verse 2 is an extended mixed chord of V which has more special Mixolydian style tastes comparing to using V7 directly.

④ . ᵇIIImaj7 in the 8th measure of Verse 2 is from III series seventh chord of a parallel minor key used as a modal interchange.

⑤. VII7 in the 5th measure of Chorus is the following V of IIIm and this is a form of V-I progression.

⑥. ♭III in the 6th measure of Chorus is from a III series chord of a parallel minor, which is a use of a modal interchange. It is also a substitution chord, with a use of a tritone substitution and what is presented along with previous and later section chords in the bass voice is a chromatic approach progression.

⑦. II7 in the 7th measure of Chorus is a V of the following V7sus4, which is an exact format of a V-I progression.

⑧. ♭VII/1 in the 7th measure of Verse 3 is a extended mixed chord of a parallel Mixolydian, which is also a practice of a modal interchange approach. And it is a mixed chord with a special key style.

⑨. IVm in the 8th measure of Verse 3 is a IV series chord generated from a parallel minor key, which is also a practice of a modal interchange approach.

⑩. ♭IIadd9/1 in 3rd measure of Verse 4 is an extended mixed chord of a parallel Phrygian, which is a practice of a modal interchange approach.

⑪. I m11 in the 5th measure of Verse 4 uses a modal interchange approach and the bass voice section continues using '1' as a bass voice.

⑫. In the very last four measures of Verse 4, a use of sustained bass notes to match with ascending and then the descending of upper voice harmony, creating different feelings of key style connection as well as emotional variations. This is the most characteristic part of the song.

Example Ⅶ
Sample chord reference song:

Everything

Misia

Form Progression

Intro → Verse 1 → Verse 2 → Bridge → Chorus 1 → Inter 1

→ Verse 2 → Bridge → Chorus 2 → Chorus 1 → Inter 2

→ Chorus 2 (to sharp a half key) → Chorus 3 → Outro

Chord Progression

Intro

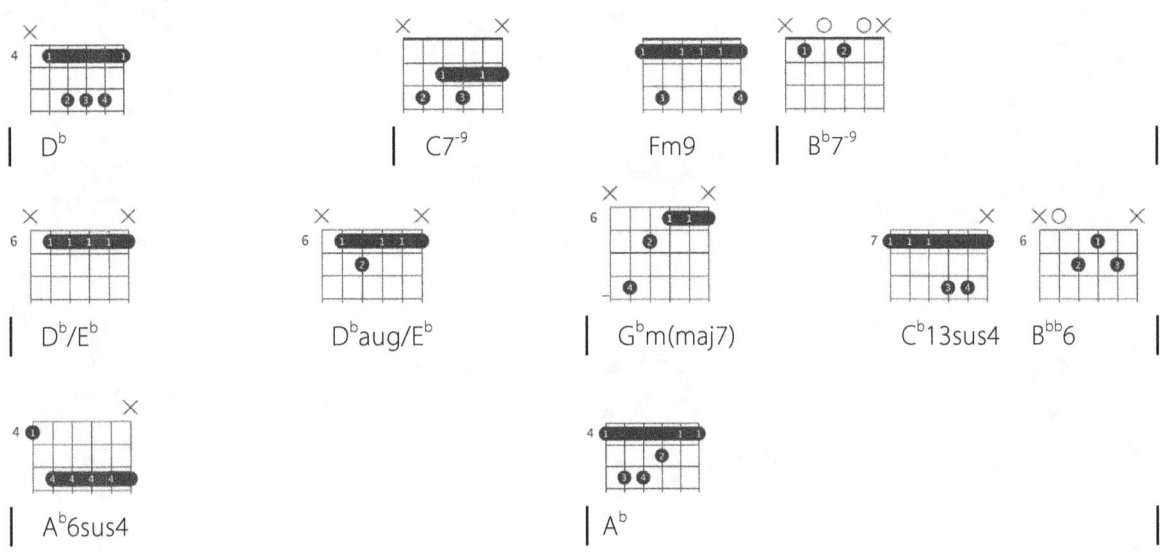

Verse 1

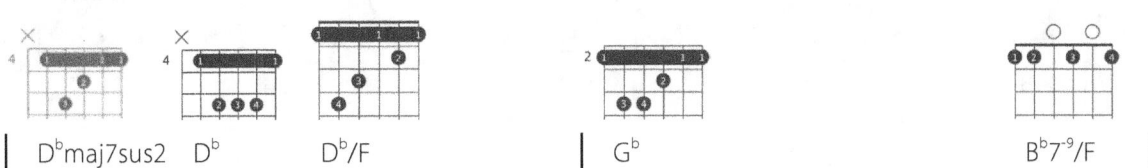

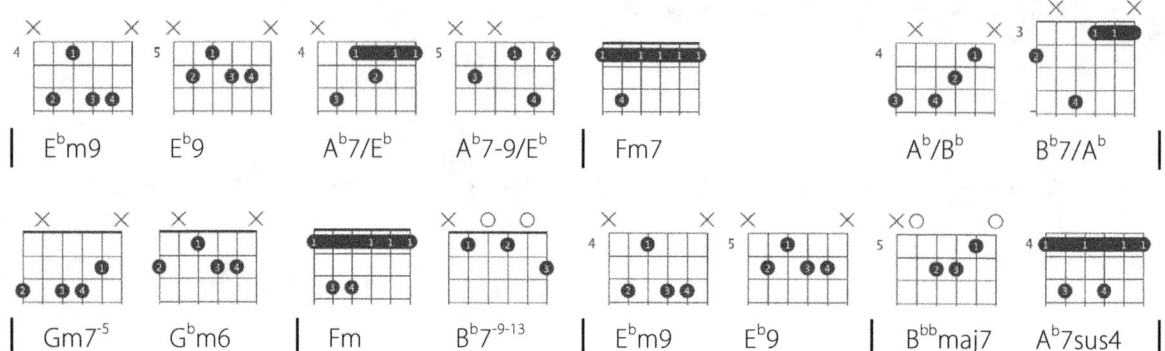

E♭m9　　E♭9　　A♭7/E♭　　A♭7-9/E♭　　Fm7　　　　　A♭/B♭　　B♭7/A♭

Gm7⁻⁵　　G♭m6　　Fm　　B♭7⁻⁹⁻¹³　　E♭m9　　E♭9　　B♭♭maj7　A♭7sus4

Verse 2

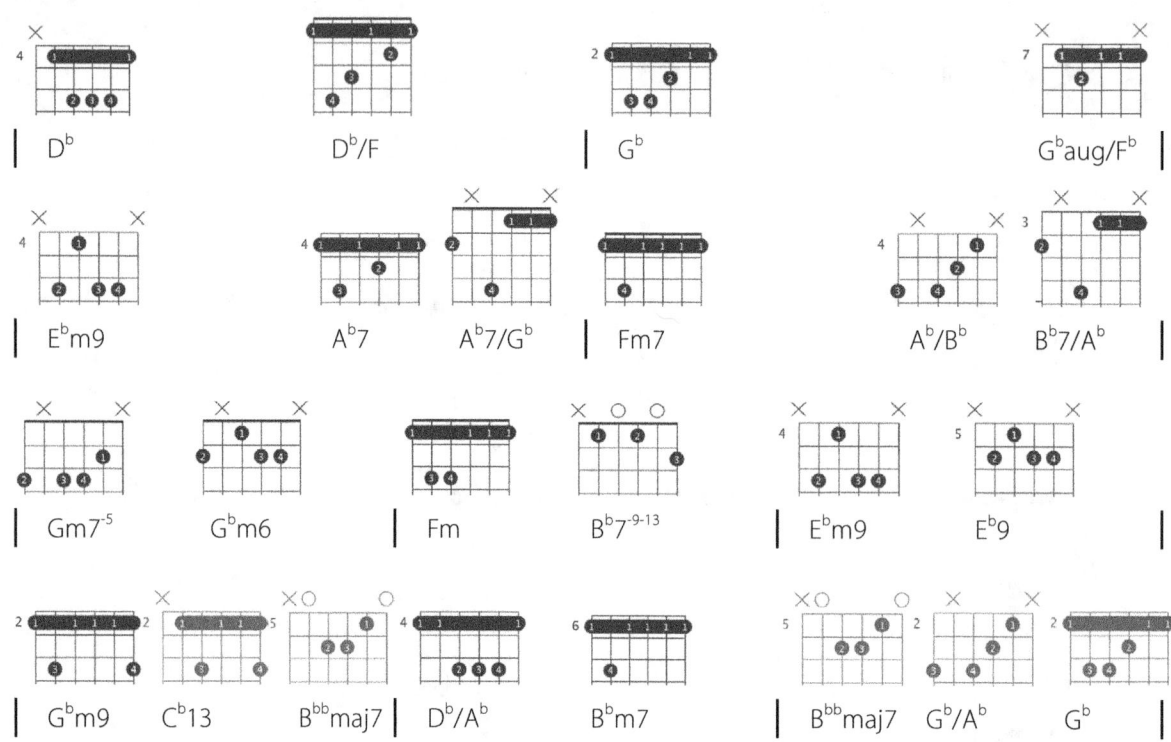

D♭　　　　D♭/F　　　　G♭　　　　　G♭aug/F♭

E♭m9　　A♭7　　A♭7/G♭　　Fm7　　　A♭/B♭　　B♭7/A♭

Gm7⁻⁵　　G♭m6　　Fm　　B♭7⁻⁹⁻¹³　　E♭m9　　E♭9

G♭m9　　C♭13　　B♭♭maj7　D♭/A♭　　B♭m7　　B♭♭maj7　G♭/A♭　　G♭

Bridge

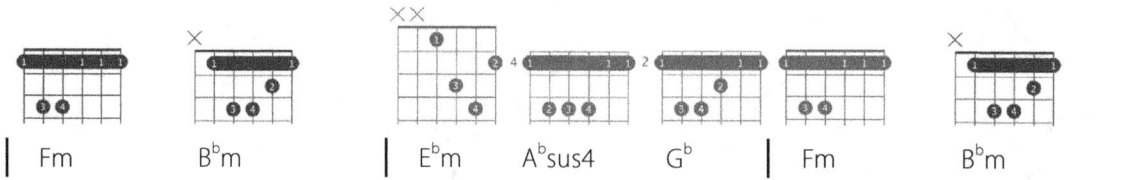

Fm　　B♭m　　E♭m　A♭sus4　G♭　　Fm　　B♭m

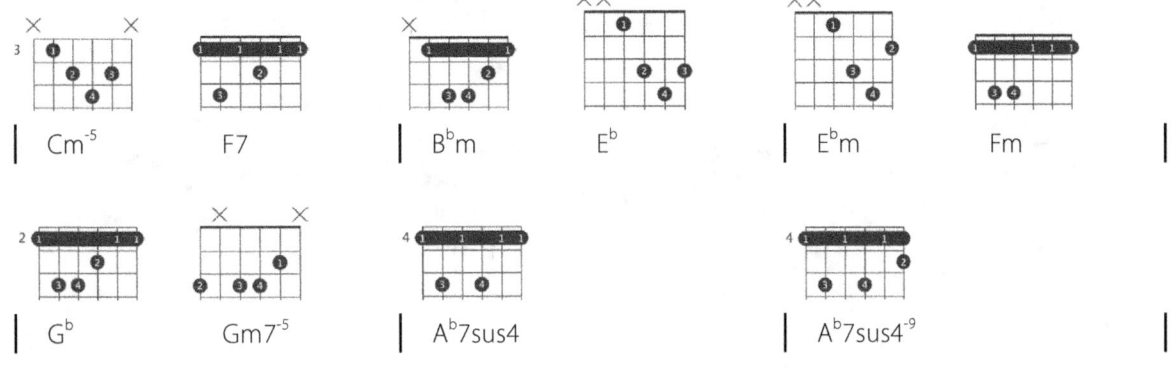

Cm⁻⁵	F7	B^bm	E^b	E^bm	Fm

G^b	Gm7⁻⁵	A^b7sus4	A^b7sus4⁻⁹

Chorus 1

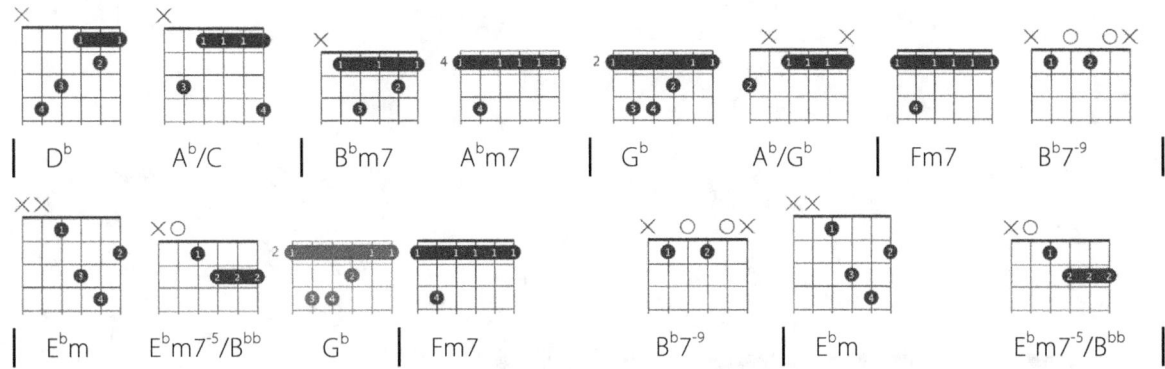

D^b	A^b/C	B^bm7	A^bm7	G^b	A^b/G^b	Fm7	B^b7⁻⁹

E^bm	E^bm7⁻⁵/B^{bb}	G^b	Fm7	B^b7⁻⁹	E^bm	E^bm7⁻⁵/B^{bb}

Inter 1

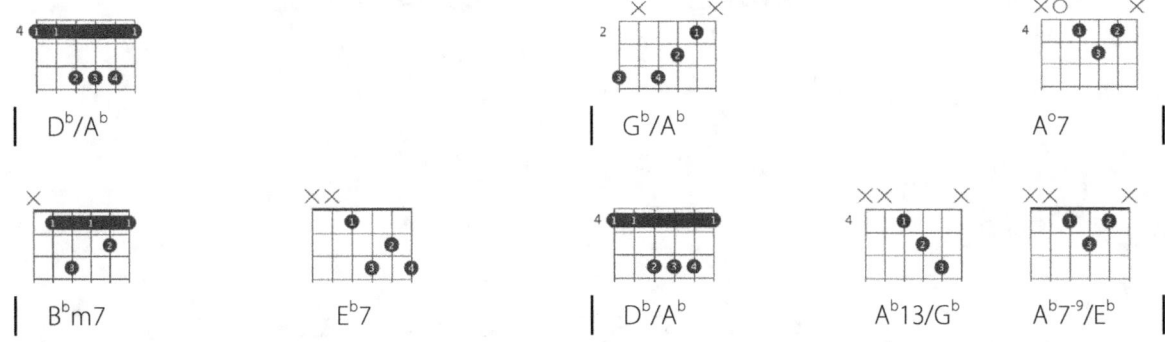

D^b/A^b	G^b/A^b	A°7

B^bm7	E^b7	D^b/A^b	A^b13/G^b	A^b7⁻⁹/E^b

Chorus 2

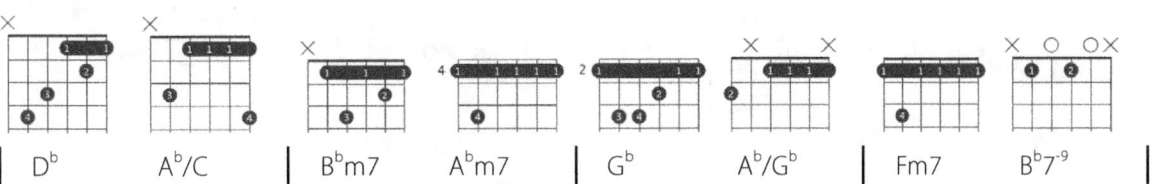

D^b	A^b/C	B^bm7	A^bm7	G^b	A^b/G^b	Fm7	B^b7⁻⁹

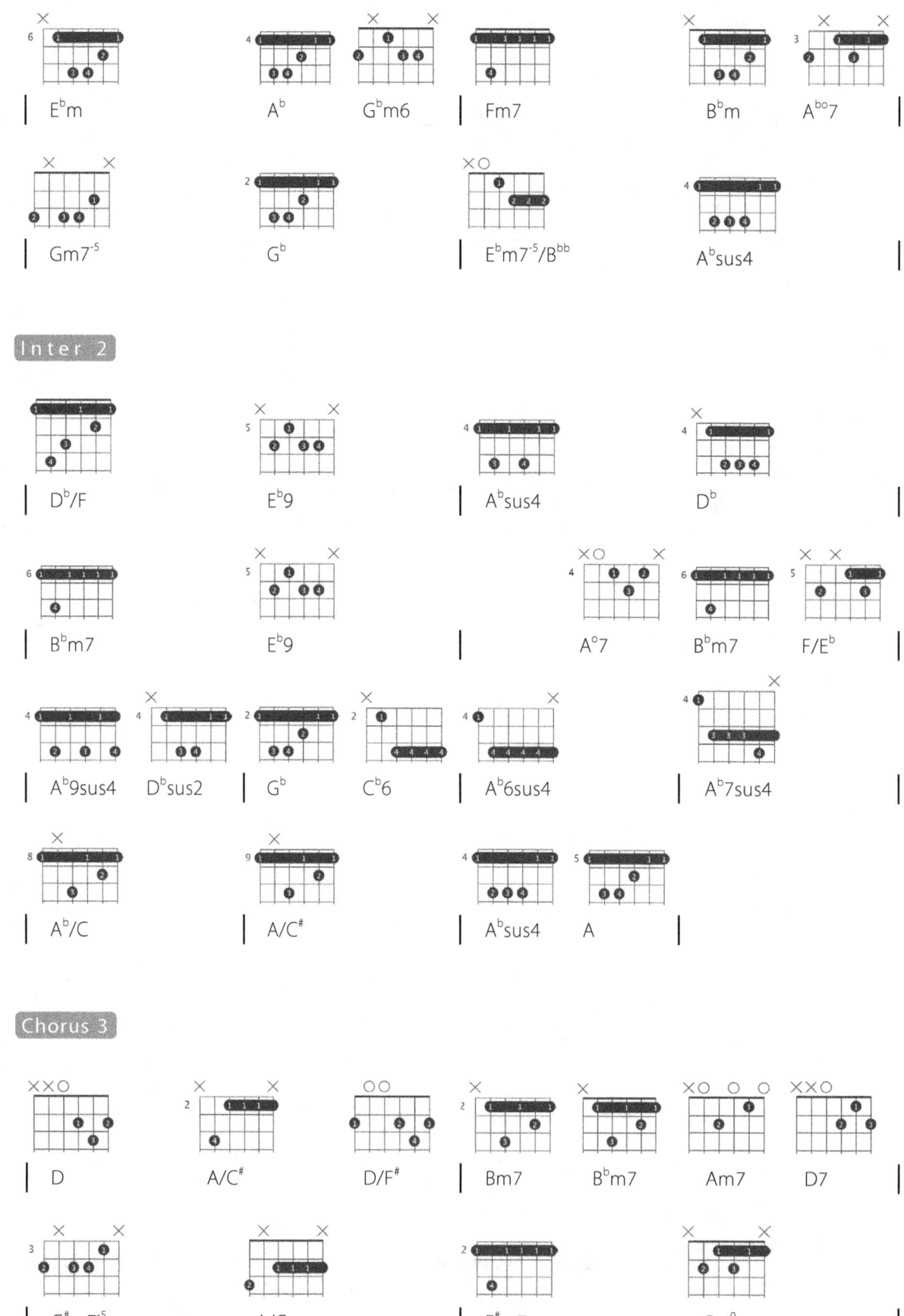

E♭m A♭ G♭m6 | Fm7 B♭m A♭o7 |

Gm7⁻⁵ G♭ | E♭m7⁻⁵/B♭♭ A♭sus4 |

Inter 2

D♭/F E♭9 | A♭sus4 D♭ |

B♭m7 E♭9 | A°7 B♭m7 F/E♭ |

A♭9sus4 D♭sus2 G♭ C♭6 A♭6sus4 A♭7sus4 |

A♭/C A/C♯ | A♭sus4 A |

Chorus 3

D A/C♯ D/F♯ | Bm7 B♭m7 Am7 D7 |

G♯m7⁻⁵ A/G | F♯m7 B7⁻⁹ |

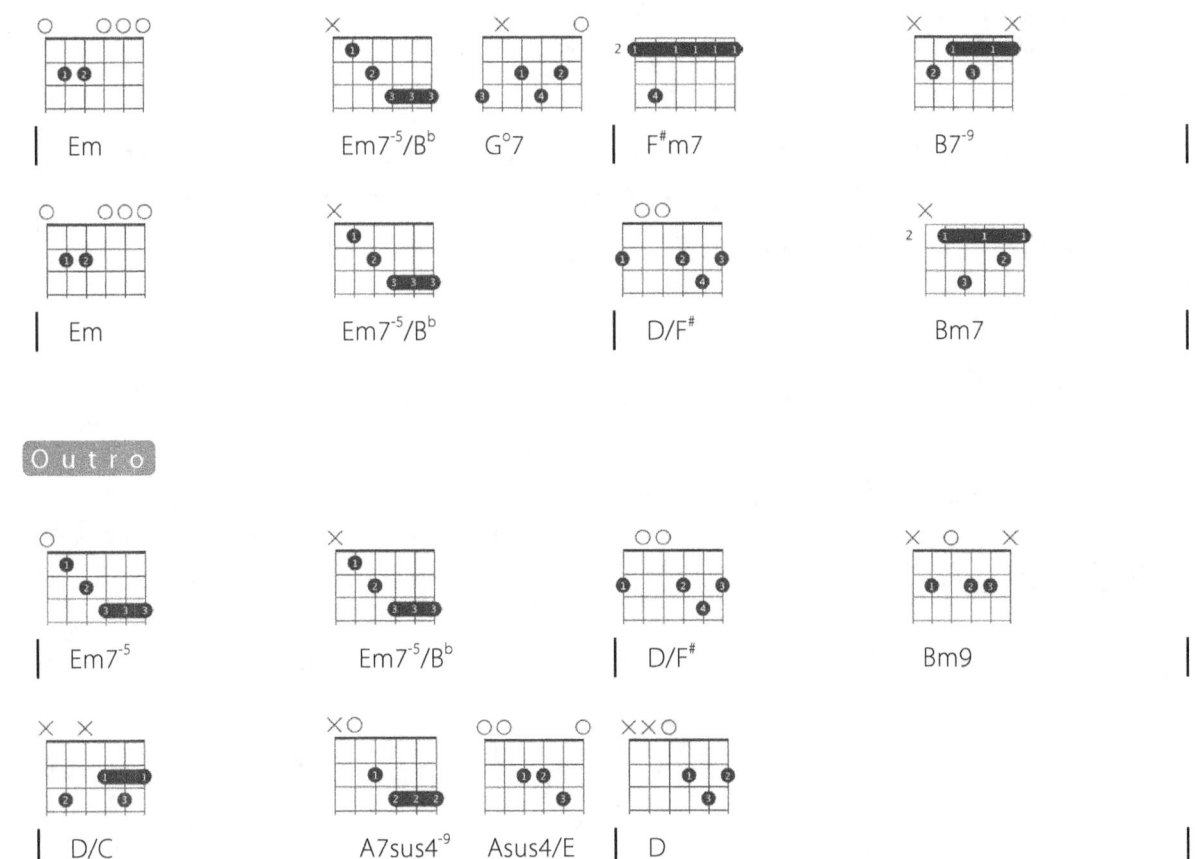

| Em | Em7⁻⁵/B♭ | G°7 | F#m7 | B7⁻⁹ | |

| Em | Em7⁻⁵/B♭ | D/F# | Bm7 | |

Outro

| Em7⁻⁵ | Em7⁻⁵/B♭ | D/F# | Bm9 | |

| D/C | A7sus4⁻⁹ Asus4/E | D | |

Analysis

This song does not contain many modulations in the key; however, it does smartly apply many chord alterations along with inversions and modal interchange, which allows musical atmospheres to be rich in layers for us to feel and to learn from.

Dᵇ key. The 5th measure of Inter 2 modulates to Gᵇ key and turns back to Dᵇ key in the 7th measure. The final chord in the last measure is being raised a half note to become a D key.

CHORD SERIES

To present in chord series ：

Intro

| I | | （FT 1）
| VII 7^{-9} III m9 | （FT 2）
VI 7^{-9} | |

| （FT 3）
| I / 2 | I aug / 2 | （FT 4）
| IV m(maj7) ᵇ VII 13sus4 | （FT 5）
ᵇ VI 6 | |

| V 6sus4 | | V | |

Verse 1

| I maj7sus2 I I / 3 | IV | （FT 6）
VI 7^{-9}/ 3 |

| II m9 （FT 7）
II 9 V 7 / 2 | （FT 8）
V 7^{-9}/ 2 | III m7 （FT 9）
V / 6 VI 7 / 5 |

| （FT 10）
IV m7^{-5} IV m6 | III m （FT 11）
VI 7^{-9-13} | II m9 （FT 12）
II 9 | ᵇ VI maj7 V 7sus4 |

Verse 2

| I | I / 3 | IV | （FT 13）
IV aug / ᵇ3 |

| II m9 V 7 V 7 / 4 | III m7 V / 6 VI 7 / 5 |

| # IV m7-5 IV m6 | III m VI 7^{-9-13} | II m9 II 9 |

| IV m9　ᵇVII 13　ᵇVI maj7 | I / 5　　　　VI m7 | ᵇVI maj7　　IV / 5　　IV |

Bridge

| III m　　　　VI m | II m　　V sus4　IV | III m　　　　VI m |

（FT 15）
| VII m⁻⁵　　　III 7 | VI m　　　　II | II m　　　　III m |

| IV　　　　♯IV m7⁻⁵ | V 7sus4　　　　　V 7sus4⁻⁹ |

Chorus 1

| I　　　V / 7 | VI m7　V m7 | IV　　　V 7/4 | III m7　VI 7⁻⁹ |

（FT 16）
| II m　II m7⁻⁵/ᵇ6　IV | III m7　　　VI 7⁻⁹ | II m　　　II m7⁻⁵/ᵇ6 |

Inter 1

（FT 17）
| I / 5　　　　　　　　　　　　| IV / 5　　　　♯V °7 |

| VI m7　　　　　II 7 | I / 5　　　V 13/4　V 7⁻⁹/2 |

Chorus 2

| I　　　V / 7 | VI m7　V m7 | IV　　　V 7/4 | III m7　VI 7⁻⁹ |

| II m　　　　V　　IV m6 | III m7　　　VI m　　　V °7 |

| ♯IV m7-5　　　　IV | II m7⁻⁵/ᵇ6　V sus4 |

Inter 2

| I / 3　　　　　II 9 | V sus4　　　　I |

（FT 18）
| VI m7　　　　II 9 | ♯V o7　VI m7　III / 2 |

| II 9sus4   V sus2 | I   IV 6 | V 6sus4 | V 7sus4 |

| V / 7 | ᵇ VI / 1 | V sus4   V | |

Chorus 3

| I   V / 7   I /3 | VI m7   ᵇ VI m7   V m7   I 7 |

| # IV m7-5   V 7/ 4 | III m7   VI 7⁻⁹ |

| II m   II m⁷⁻⁵ / ᵇ6   IV °7 | III m7   VI 7⁻⁹ |

| II m   II m⁷⁻⁵ / ᵇ6 | I / 3   VI m7 |

Outro

| II m⁷⁻⁵   II m⁷⁻⁵ / ᵇ6 | I / 3   VI m9 |

(FT 20)

| I / ᵇ7   V 7sus4⁻⁹   V sus4 / 2 | I |

REMARKS

①. VII7⁻⁹ , the 2nd chord of Intro is the following V series minor ninth chord of III m9.

②. VI7⁻⁹, the 4th chord of Intro is the following V series minor ninth mixed chord of II series

③. I / 2 in the 4th measure of Intro is from the II series of an extended chord, by taking off the 3rd note of a chord and allowing the upper voices to become a comprising note of I . And this becomes a more ambiguous mixed chord. By looking at this chord combination alone, you can see quite a rich color in a Mixolydian key style. And the following is the altered chord of the upper voices.

④. IVm(maj7) in the 5th measure of Intro uses a IV series chord from a modal interchange of parallel natural minor key and in which, the 7th note of a natural minor key was turned to a maj7 to emphasize colors of a major key. Meanwhile, the use of inversion produces different feelings for bass voices.

⑤. ♭VII13sus4 and ♭VI6 in the 5th measure of Intro are from modal interchange of parallel natural minor key

⑥. VI7^{-9} / 3, the 2nd chord of Verse 1 in the 2nd measure is the 2nd inversion of a V series minor ninth chord of the following IIm9

⑦. II9 in the 3rd measure of Verse 1 is the following V of V7 / 2.

⑧. V7^{-9} / 2 in the 3d measure of Verse 1 uses V series of minor ninth chord of parallel harmonic minor key with a modal interchange approach.

⑨. V / 6 and VI7 / 5 in the 4th measure of Verse 1 and #IVm7-5 in the 5th measure forms chromatic descending in the treble voice section. And the two slash chords in the previous section progress by using VI series chord in a dominant seventh chord form. V / 6 can be seen as a VI7sus4 and VI7 / 5 is the 3rd inversion of VI7 without proceeding to any resolution in the end; it however, progresses to the next chord along with a chromatic alteration.

⑩. #IVm7-5 in the 5th measure of Verse 1 uses IV series chord of parallel Lydian with a modal interchange approach, and the following IVm6 uses IV series chord of a parallel natural minor.

⑪. VI7^{-9-13} in the 6th measure of Verse 1 is V series of the following IIm9.

⑫. II9 in the 7th measure of Verse 1 is V of V7sus4 in the 8th measure in the back, and in between them, a VI series ♭VImaj7 of parallel minor key is added as a bridge chord of chromatic approach in the bass voice.

⑬ IV aug / ^{b}3 in the 2nd measure of Verse 2 is a mixed chord of an augmented chord, among them, the bass voice and the comprising notes can contain chromatic effects along with the following chords.

⑭ In addition to modal interchange, IVm9 and ^{b}VII13 in the 8th measure of Verse 2 also contain a II → V relation. This measure lengthens the time of II9 in the 7th measure and moves forward to I / 5 of the 9th measure.

⑮ VIIm^{-5}, III7 and VIm in the 4th and 5th measures of Bridge, is a II → V → I relation of a minor key, VIm is connected to a II in the back and it is also a II → V relation.

⑯ II m7^{-5} / ^{b}6 in the 5th measure of Chorus 1 is a modal interchange approach using II series chord of a parallel minor key and it's a second inversion.

⑰ The diminished seventh chord $^\#$V^{o}7 in the 2nd measure of Inter 1 uses a chromatic approach in bass voice to reach a bridge chord of VIm.

⑱ III / 2 bass voice in the 4th measure of Inter 2 forms a V → I relation with the following II 9sus4 modulating to G^b key. Therefore, function wise, it is a secondary dominant chord, not a inversion chord. After analyzing the previous and later chord comprising notes, you can discover it allows chromatic alterations in the voices.

⑲ In the 11th measure of Inter 2, we directly use a chromatic approach raising to V series of a D key to conduct a key modulation.

Your Training Notebook On Pop Music Special Chord Progressions

⑳ I / ♭7 in the 3rd measure of Outro is not an inversion of an I series seventh chord; instead, it is a ♭VII extended chord of VII series natural minor key with a modal interchange approach. The chord is applied and used in a mixed chord form and therefore to form a colorful atmosphere of a Lydian key style.

When you see a slash chord (the so-called slash chord), how do you identify whether it is an inversion chord or a mixed chord?

Frankly, this is not difficult at all. As long as you take the upper chords and directly replace them in progression and try playing them out. If it sounds like about the same as the original feelings and atmospheres, then it should belong to an inversion chord; if its sounds seem to be quite different in tastes, then it belongs to a mixed chord. Often time, feelings of a mixed chord is more like an extension or an altered chord of root. Its taste is more ambiguous and not so stable. There will also be more room to connect to many other chords, and this is usually used in other music types similar to Fusion.

Chapter of Analysis & Integration

Now are you more familiar with the previous chord progression ? Then let's integrate techniques in these songs.

Please remember to integrate these techniques as well as the analyses as they often symbolize elements which make the sound be good and dramatically. They are often used merely to represent elements of good sounding and tensions. We learn about these to add more tools in our music learning experiences and this doesn't mean that we can only use these tools, not necessarily suggesting that the music is guaranteed to sound nice with these tools because our ears will still be the fairest judge in the end.

Everyone owns the same tools, however, his presentations would vary from one person to another and we can experience more in these songs !

Diatonic Triad

This is the basic chord within the key. Different keys have their own belonging basic diatonic chords, which are quite different from other keys. However, their comprising format is all the same; therefore, they can be presented with chord series (or the Roman numeric symbols). I series means the 1st chord within the key and etc..

Series	I	II	III	IV	V	VI	VII
C Key	C	Dm	Em	F	G	Am	Bm^{-5}
G Key	G	Am	Bm	C	D	Em	F$^{\#}$m^{-5}
Direct presentation	I	II m	III m	IV	V	VI m	VII m^{-5}

Direct presentation uses Roman numeric symbols to replace numbers in numbered musical notation, and this avoids confusions between chord names and the comprising numbers on the right hand side (-5, sus4...).

Inversion Chord

The presentation form of an inversion chord is a type of slash chord; the upper one is the chord and the bass voice part is the comprising notes of other chords other than the roots. The 3rd note in bass voice is called a first inversion, and 5th note is called a second inversion in the bass voice. If there are four seventh chords for the chord comprising notes, then there will be a third inversion.

An inversion chord is often used for:

①. Bridge.

②. Reducing big interval jumps for the bass voice（big jumps on fret position can be avoided upon chord-changing on the guitar）

③. Designing melodic lines of bass voices, conjunct motion or effects chromatic approach.

In C key the most commonly seen are G/B, C/E, C/G and etc. Such as progressions below：

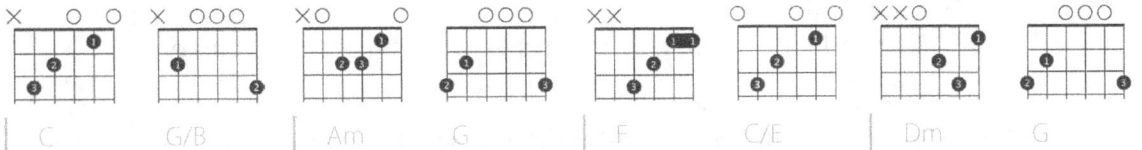

| C | G/B | Am | G | F | C/E | Dm | G |

The bass voice has melodic lines of a diatonic descending scale. And certainly, if it would be all right to only play the original chord in the upper layer and this is so because the main function is from a root position of the original position. You can try to play this and compare the effects on your own.

In the previous songs, except 《Example IV: I Just Can't Stop Loving you》, every other song has used an inversion chord and this is very often seen. Please slowly feel and experience their differences as well as the effects.

Mixed Chord

The presentational form of a mixed chord is also a type of slash chord. What it is different from an inversion chord is: the upper chord notes are from non-chord tones or extended notes of the bass voice which is used as root, or the available notes from a scale. And it may possibly be for proceeding an altered chromatic approach with the front and back voices and thus forms a chord. This type of chord usually takes out the original 3rd note of the chord, so upon use, the feeling is a bit more ambiguous. Although the form of upper voice is comprised of another chord, but the main chord function still mainly focuses on a chord position which belongs to bass chords at the bottom. Many key modes and harmonies usually appear in this form.

There are similar functions of a mixed chord and an inversion chord, they are often used for

①. Bridge.

②. Using this to design melodic lines of chord progression, conjunct motion or effects of a chromatic approach.

③. Key modulation.

④. To produce a feeling of indecisive, pending and unstable.

The most commonly seen is F/G, D/C and etc. in C key, such as the progression below:

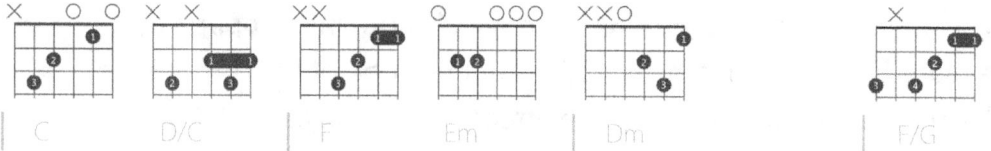

| C | D/C | F | Em | Dm | F/G |

In regards to the judgments of an inversion chord or a mixed chord, please refer to footnotes in analysis in the previous 《Example VII: Everything》 （p.61）

In the previous repertories, mixed chords appear in:

《Example IV : I Just Can't Stop Loving you–Chorus & Bridge》、《Example V: Say Yes》、《Example VI : Evergreen》、《Example VII: Everything》

Modal Interchange

A modal interchange is to take all chords in a parallel key for an equal position replacement or a method of a direct use. And in addition to parallel minor key which we are all familiar with, there are chords of other parallel key forms that can be used with a modal interchange approach.

The so-called a 'key mode' is to follow each note on a natural scale as a tonic and to form a scale. There are 7 modes including Ionian, Dorian, Phrygian, Lydian, Mixolydian, Aeolian and Locrian respectively, and among them, Ionian which uses the 1st note as a tonic is similar to a major key scale. And an Aeolian which uses the 6th note as a tonic is similar to a minor key scale.

Tonic	Mode	Scales	Format of scale structure (Tonic is '1')						
C	C Ionian	C D E F G A B	1	2	3	4	5	6	7
D	D Dorian	D E F G A B C	1	2	$^b3$	4	5	6	$^b7$
E	E Phrygian	E F G A B C D	1	$^b2$	$^b3$	4	5	$^b6$	$^b7$
F	F Lydian	F G A B C D E	1	2	3	$^\#4$	5	6	7
G	G Mixolydian	G A B C D E F	1	2	3	4	5	6	$^b7$
A	A Aeolian	A B C D E F G	1	2	$^b3$	4	5	$^b6$	$^b7$
B	B Locrian	B C D E F G A	1	$^b2$	$^b3$	4	$^b5$	$^b6$	$^b7$

Based on scales of each mode, with an addition of a natural minor key, a harmonic minor key and a melodic minor scale to form a diatonic harmony of each series can be presented as the chart below:

Serise	I	II	III	IV	V	VI	VII
Natural minor	I m	II m^{-5}	^{b}III	IV m	V m	^{b}VI	^{b}VII
Harmonic minor	I m	II m^{-5}	^{b}III $^+$	IV m	V	^{b}VI	VII m^{-5}
Melodic minor	I m	II m	^{b}III $^+$	IV	V	VI m^{-5}	VII m^{-5}
Dorian	I m	II m	^{b}III	IV	V m	VI m^{-5}	^{b}VII
Phrygian	I m	^{b}II	^{b}III	IV m	V m^{-5}	^{b}VI	^{b}VII m
Lydian	I	II	III m	IV m	V	VI m	VII m
Mixolydian	I	II m	III m^{-5}	IV	V m	VI m	^{b}VII
Locrian	I m	^{b}II	^{b}III m	IV m	^{b}V	^{b}VI	^{b}VII m

To view from a triad form, there are many repeated chords; however, if you see this in a seventh chord form, you are able to see the differences more obviously upon use:

Series	I	II	III	IV	V	VI	VII
Natural minor	I m7	II m7^{-5}	✓ ^{b}III maj7	✓ IV m7	V m7	^{b}VI maj7	✓ ^{b}VII 7
Harmonic minor	✓ I m(maj7)	✓ II m7^{-5}	^{b}III maj7$^+$	IV m7	✓ V 7	^{b}VI maj7	✓ VII °7
Melodic minor	I m(maj7)	II m7	^{b}III maj7$^+$	IV 7	V 7	VI m7^{-5}	VII m7^{-5}
Dorian	I m7	II m7	III maj7	✓ IV 7	V m7	✓ VI m7^{-5}	✓ VII maj7
Phrygian	I m7	✓ ^{b}II maj7	✓ ^{b}III 7	IV m7	✓ V m7^{-5}	✓ ^{b}VI maj7	✓ ^{b}VII m7
Lydian	I maj7	✓ II 7	III m7	✓ $^\#$IV m7^{-5}	✓ V maj7	VI m7	VII m7
Mixolydian	✓ I 7	II m7	✓ III m7^{-5}	IV maj7	✓ V m7	VI m7	✓ ^{b}VII maj7
Locrian	✓ I m7^{-5}	^{b}II maj7	✓ ^{b}III m7	IV m7	✓ ^{b}V maj7	✓ ^{b}VI 7	^{b}VII m7

Chords with check-marks are regularly chords used for a modal interchange. And certainly all these organized charts are for your references. In practice, the use of a modal interchange will still mainly consider feelings of listening.

Generally speaking:

①. In major key music, it often performs a modal interchange with chords of a Natural minor key , Lydian and Mixolydian.

②. In minor key music, it often performs a modal interchange with chords of a Harmonic minor key , Melodic minor key and Dorian.

③. If an ' I m6 ' appears, then it belongs to a modal interchange of a minor key, using 6th note as a differentiation with a ' I m(maj7)' harmonic minor key.

④. ^{b}II maj7 , ^{b}VI7 and ^{b}VII7 often appear in cadences, and among them, to the original key ^{b}II and ^{b}VI7, it is a type of augmented sixth chord.

⑤. The use of V m7 is often seen to be from a Mixolydian, and not a natural minor key （which is also often treated as 2 in 251 progression）.

⑥. If a IVm6 or IVm(maj7) appear, this often belongs to an IVm7 form, however, IVm(maj7) gives more of a major key feeling due to its major seventh is the 3rd note in a major key scale.

⑦. A V7^{-9} is often followed by a II m7^{-5} ， and at this time, it is from a harmonic minor key modal interchange.

⑧. Mixed chords are often from a modal interchange approach. For example: D/C, is a mixed chord from C Lydian and can be seen as a presentation form of a Cmaj7($^{\#}$11).

The IV series chord in a song usually uses a modal interchange form ：

In fact, in regards to a matter like 'how to use a chord?' we don't spend too much time here to explain as this is all from the analysis of music and song. And everyone may possibly have his own ideas and methods; therefore, to experience and analyze this from listening to music, you can really learn well and also to have an easier time remember it. Thus, here I share only a big picture of a modal interchange. Each of you can also try and experience more on song analysis upon composition and song arrangement.

Of course if you want to learn detailed harmony and music theory, please search for other specialized teaching materials on harmony and theory.

And of the song list from the previous section, each song has used a modal interchange approach. About modal interchange parts in each song, please refer to the analysis section after each song list.

Sustained Note

The use of a sustained note has nearly no limitations, and to view this from the frequency of use, the most frequently appearing sustained notes are the tonic and dominant notes, which allows stability of key and is mostly used in bass voice. Chords of upper voice are most commonly used as chords within a key in the beginning and the end, and sometime in the middle section, dissonant chords of sustained notes will be used as an effect of tensions. Such dramatic tension formation and resolution are often thought to be a good method.

And two or three sustained notes sometimes may show simultaneously.

The appearing of a sustained note is often accompanied by an inversion or a mixed chord. It belongs to a type method of a vertical direction consideration.

Below is an example of C key which uses C as a tonic sustained note.

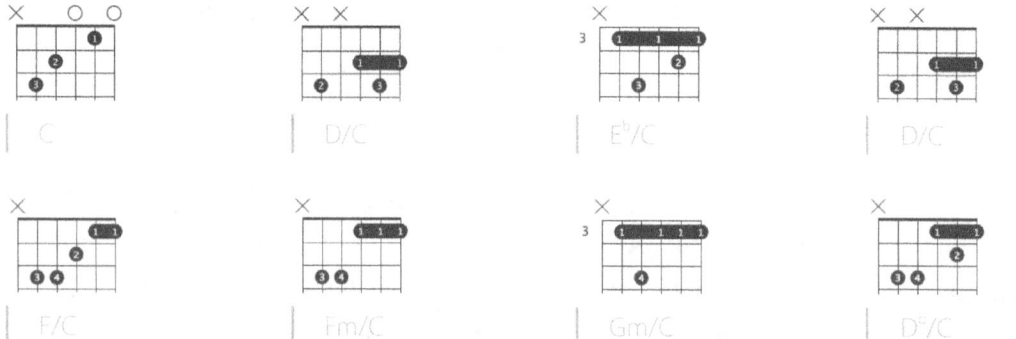

In the previous songs, sustained notes have been used in:

《Example II : Somewhere Over The Rainbow – Intro, Chorus》、《Example V : Say Yes – Intro, Verse 2, Inter 1, Chorus 3 End》、《Example VI : Evergreen – Intro, Verse 1, Verse 4》、《Example VII : Everything – Inter 1, Inter 2》 have relatively shorter sustained notes.

- 5 - 1   **Progression**

A 2-5-1 progression is for the three continuous chords, the relation would be Ⅱ → Ⅴ → Ⅰ , and this temporary relation may possibly be just a 2-5 or a 5-1, the key point is that there is a 5 （Ⅴ） existing in the relation.

The Ⅴ in here can be called as a sub-dominant or a secondary dominant chord. It is considered as a dominant chord of a target chord Ⅰ , and basically its root needs notes from a scale within the key. Therefore, the Ⅱ,Ⅲ,Ⅳ,Ⅴ and Ⅵ series of a key can generate their own sub-dominant chords. Also, sub-dominant chord of Ⅶ series is not quite often used because its root of a perfect 5th is not a note within the key. Taking C key as one example, it is as below:

Secondary chord （Ⅴ）	Target chord （Ⅰ）
A or A7	Dm
B or B7	Em
C or C7	F
D or D7	G
E or E7	Am

A secondary dominant chord usually uses its seventh chord to better perform its functions in a more obvious form and this is because the structure of a dominant seven chord within a key chord can only exist on a Ⅴ series.

2 of a 2-5-1 is a relative Ⅱm chord, which is also a minor third form. Therefore, taking C key as one example, the use of a 2-5-1 chord is generally as below:

Relative II m	Secondary dominant chord (V)	Target chord (I)
Em or Em7	A or A7	Dm
F#m or F#m7	B or B7	Em
Gm or Gm7	C or C7	F
Am or Am7	D or D7	G
Bm or Bm7	E or E7	Am

Speaking of the use, we can often discover that if a target I is in a form of a minor third chord then the relative II m often uses II m7^{-5} of a minor key form. It's like a minor key form of a 2-5-1 progression, II m7^{-5} → V 7 → I m.

Example:

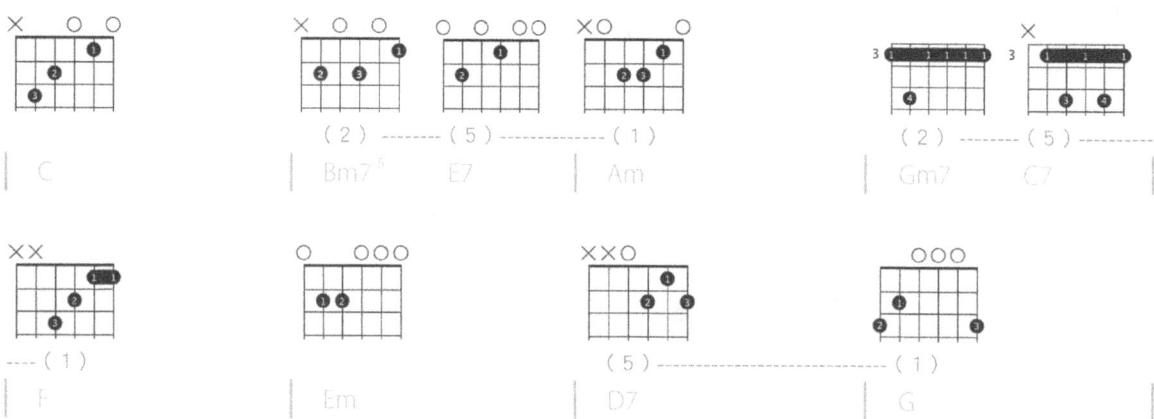

In the previous songs, except 《Example I : Beautiful》, other ones have all adopted a 2-5-1 progression or partial 2-5-1 progression, and this is also a very commonly seen use. Please proceed to analysis section in the back of each song for further understanding and learning.

If one song has many 2-5-1 blocks which belong to different keys, then that is music with multiple keys. In Jazz music, songs of polytonality appear often.

Diminished Seventh Chord

A diminished seventh chord is not like other seventh chords adding a major seventh or a minor seventh to the original chord and then become a diminished seventh chord, however, its seventh note must be a note from a diminished note. That is, a diminished chord plus a diminished seventh note then it becomes a diminished seventh chord.

Viewing from the structure, it is exactly 1 ^{b}3 ^{b}5 ^{bb}7. We can discover one special area within them, and that is what is in between the neighboring comprising notes are all one interval of a minor third. And therefore, its inversion would be equal to another diminished seventh chord. That is to say that four diminished seventh chords with different names are actually the same chord.

$$C°7 = E^{b}°7 = G^{b}°7 = B^{bb}°7(A°7)$$
$$C^{\#}°7 = E°7 = G°7 = B^{b}°7$$
$$D°7 = F°7 = A^{b}°7 = C^{b}°7(B°7)$$

And as a result, after summing up all the diminished seventh chords, only three types are left.

For characteristics of the interval, it makes a diminished seventh chord to sound quite ambiguous and unstable, however, because of this, it can almost be resolved to any other chords without sounding strange. And of course, in a real hands on experience, it still needs our ears for a feeling judgment upon use.

This characteristic are used in the areas of:

①. Bridge.

②. Key modulation.

③. Chromatic approach.

(That is a chromatic approach of bass voices ascending or descending to a target chord, for instance, placing a ^{b}II°7 between I and IIm.)

④. Dominant chord (V series) substitution.

(a dominant minor ninth chord of a harmonic minor is comprised of : 5 7 2 4 ^{b}6, after eliminating the root then it becomes a structure of a diminished seventh chord.)

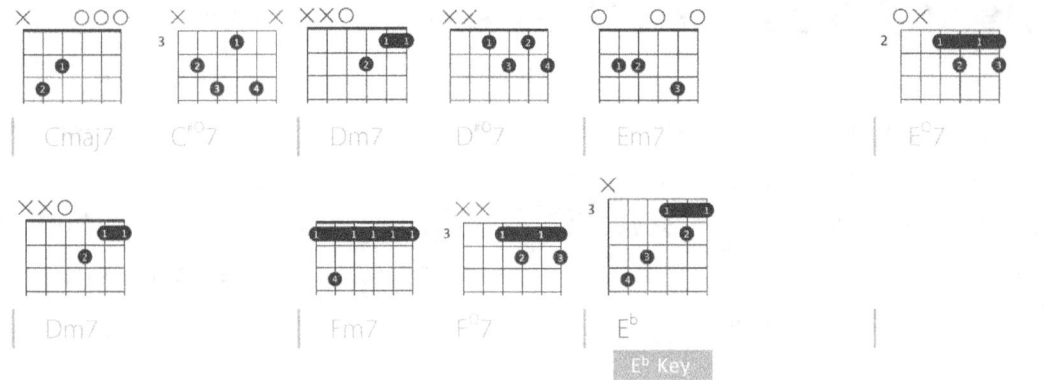

Previous sample songs which use a diminished seventh chord are:

《Example II : Somewhere Over The Rainbow – Verse, Chorus》、《Example III : She - Verse》、《Example V : Say Yes–Chorus》、《Example VII : Everything–Verse 1, Inter 1, Chorus 2, Chorus 3》

Tritone Substituion

This means to use $^b\mathrm{II}$ this chord to replace V of $\mathrm{V} \to \mathrm{I}$ which is being used originally. Generally speaking, a seventh chord form is used for a replacement and the reason is because of their structures below:

Taking C key as one example:

$$^b\mathrm{II}\,7 = {}^b2\;4\;{}^b6\;{}^b1$$
$$\mathrm{V}\,7 = 5\;7\;2\;4$$

They all have 4 and 7 (^{b}1) these two keys and in addition to the unstable interval（Tritone）of these two keys which needs to be resolved, the 7th note is the leading tone with a tendency to move toward to 1st for a resolution. And there is also a tendency for the 4th note to move to the 3rd note for a resolution.

Therefore, the two chords have the same function, $\mathrm{V}\,7 \to \mathrm{I}$ is able to become $^b\mathrm{II}\,7 \to \mathrm{I}$ as a replacement.

Taking the previous 2-5-1 progression, with a use of tritone substitution, it then becomes a 2-b2-1 progression. They are able to exist in a partial form of a 2-b2 or a b2-1.

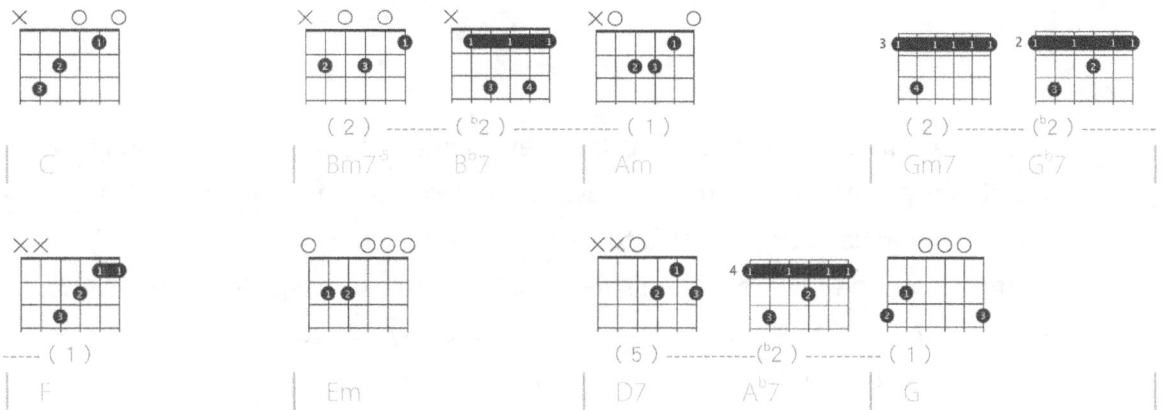

In the previous songs, 《Example VI : Evergreen – Chorus》 should be the one uses this approach. However, its ♭Ⅲ does not appear in a seventh chord form, therefore, its function to temporarily replace a dominant chord is relatively weak.

Extended & Altered Dominant Chord

Because chord progression's function wise, a dominant chord contains instability and a feeling which need to be resolved, it enables more alterations: in addition to the seventh chord, the extended ninth chord, eleventh chord and thirteen chord, an altered dominant chord instead usually has changes such as one sharp or one flat semitone on the 5th and 9th notes.

A dominant ninth chord includes a dominant major ninth chord of a major key and a dominant minor ninth chord of a minor key. Generally speaking, a dominant minor ninth is a lot more useful than a dominant major ninth chord as it can resolve progressions to a major key or a minor key of a tonic chord. However, a dominant major ninth is not suitable to be resolved to the tonic chord of a minor key.

Dominant minor ninth （ V 7⁻⁹ ） → I

→ I m

Dominant major ninth （ V 9 ） → I

✗ → I m

    This feature is related to a modal interchange approach, and is also related to a dominant minor ninth with a removal of the root to become a diminished seventh chord. If you can combine this to the second dominant chord of a 2-5-1 progression, then there will be special feelings in the song. We can see many uses like this in 《Example VII : Everything》 , specially it is commonly used in a dominant chord of II series:

III m → VI 7⁻⁹ → II m

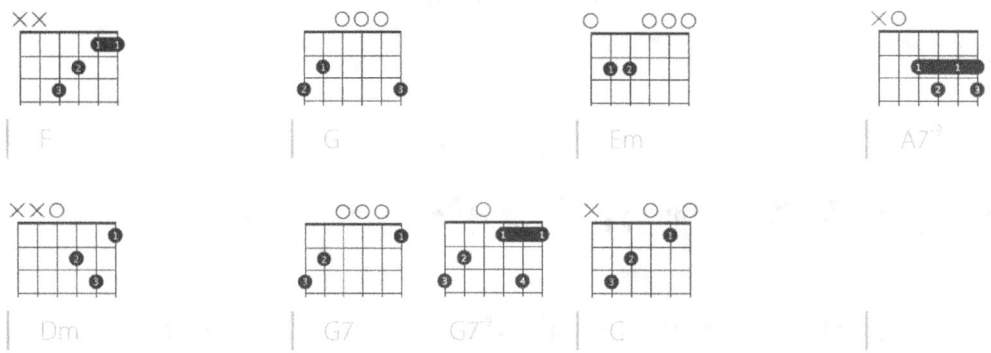

| F | G | Em | A7⁻⁹ | |

| Dm | G7 | G7⁻⁹ | C | |

    And the dominant chord of an altered 5th will also be represented as ♭13 note form (that is a #5), a ♭5 note will also appear in a form of #11. In 《Example VI : Everything》 a similar chord structure is also used. We can experience and try this method more.

A dominant chord which contains a #9 note would less likely to appear in popular music, however it is easier to be found in pop music that contains some jazz elements.

Modulation

To see whether there's a need for a key modulation in the middle of one song, there are many points you will need to consider including ranges of human voice, producing clear and obvious sections, or an increase of tensions in a song, changes of emotions and atmospheres and etc. And certainly, a use of key modulation doesn't necessarily mean it's better or to increase a tension of songs.

Key modulation can be divided into a neighboring key modulation or a distant key modulation. After modulating into a key in which the interval between each other is the only one sharp or one flat key away and then it is called a neighboring modulation key. If it's more than 2 intervals and above that, then it is called a distance key modulation.

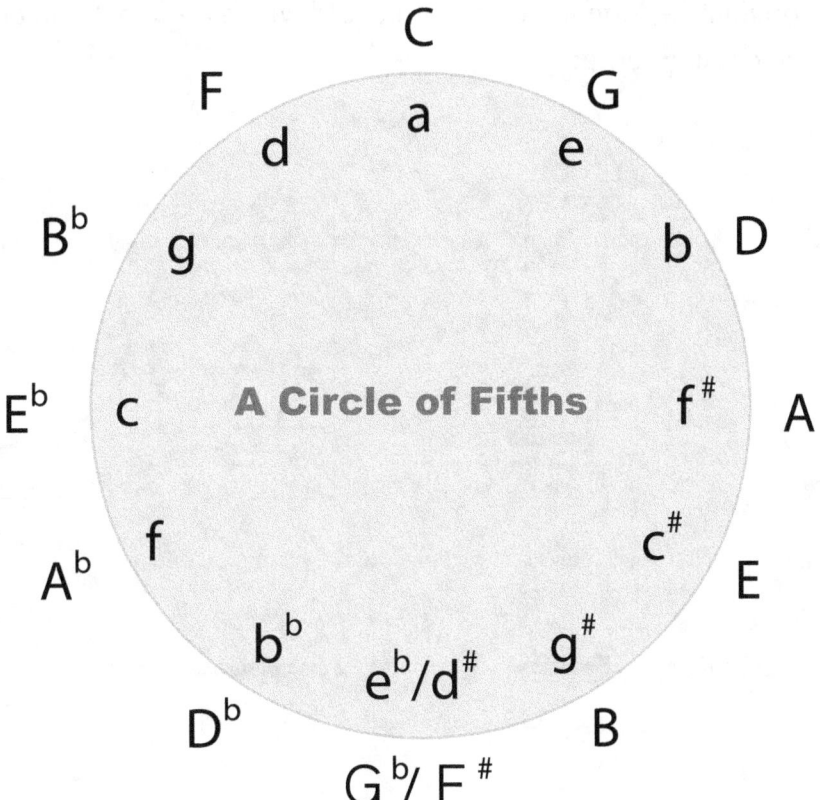

By using a Circle of Fifths to clearly represent that, taking C key as a center point and then modulates to the 5 keys in the surrounding area （G major key, F major key, A minor key, E minor key and D minor key） and this is a nearby key for a key modulation.

Methods of Key Modulation:

1. Common Chord: it is often via a common chord of two keys as an important key chord to connect a modulation, the number of a common chord is not limited to one only, after entering into a new key, a dominant chord of a new key is often being connected, and then progresses to the tonic chord of a new key （common key chord→ V → I ） to complete key modulation. This method is often to be a chord obtained through the original key modal interchange as the next common chord progression connection of the next key. Or it can be a common chord after a key modal interchange of an original key chord and that of a new key, or a common chord after a key modal interchange of a new key and an old key.

In addition, there's a method of using enharmonic common chords of a key modulation. It's like via features of a diminished seventh chord or that of a original key dominant seventh chord which is equal to an altered chord of a new key （Augmented 6th）.

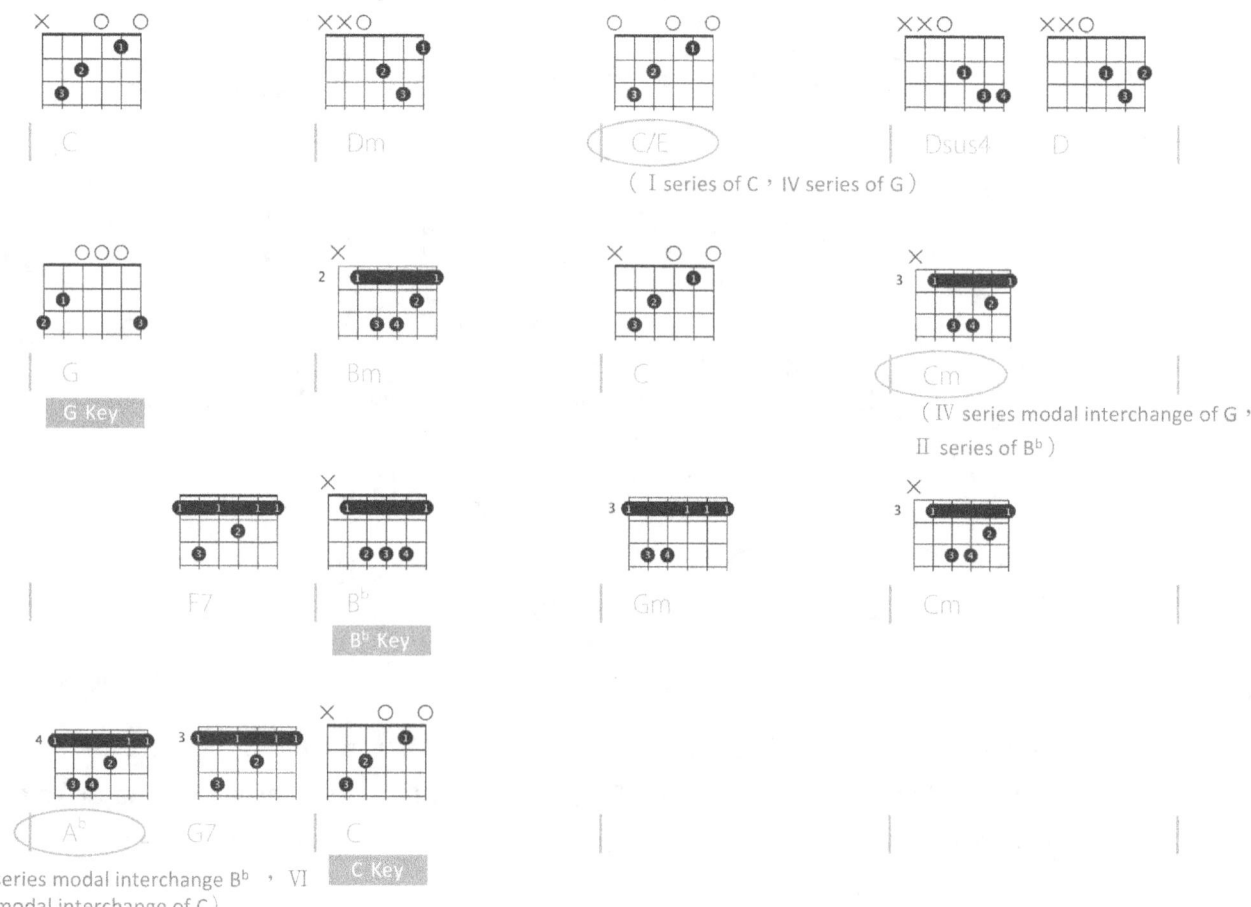

Your Training Notebook On Pop Music Special Chord Progressions

Of the previous repertoires which adopt this method for a key modulation have included:

《Example III : She》, 《Example IV : I Just Can't Stop Loving you》, 《Example V : Say Yes》, and 《Example VI : Everything》.

2. Direction Key Modulation: Of such method, what is with a better effect often time is that a major key modulates to a perfect 5th minor key at the bottom, or a minor key modulates to the upper perfect 5th major key. If viewing the minor key with a relative major key, then this would be equivalent to a nice exchanging modulation effect between a major key itself and a major key with a major 3rd interval.

Of the previous repertories that follow this key modulation method have included: 《Example III : She》

3. Diminished Seven Chord: another type is through comprising notes of an altered chromatic method (to take one of the notes for a descending semitone, and the 3 notes among them for a ascending semitone), allowing these to enter of a dominant seventh chord of a new key and then proceeds to a key modulation.

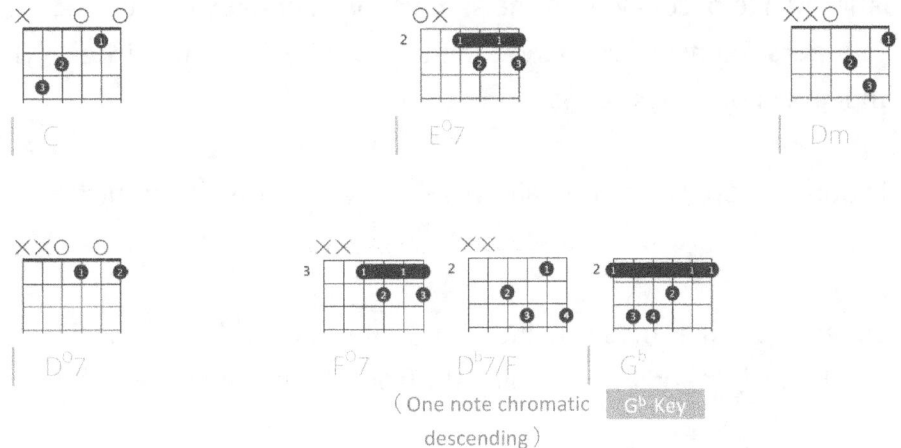

Often time, the most commonly seen key modulation approach in popular music is mainly the common chord and direct key modulation approach. Regardless of which method, the most important thing is the better sounding, and smoother it is; the better. And you should also avoid an out of pitch sounding, and because of this, inversion chords are also used upon a key modulation for a more fluent modulation experience.

And often time, the performance of a main melody upon a key modulation will also affect the fluency of a modulation, and sometimes, you will feel it's strange when you listen to chord progressions of a key modulation only; however, after adding the main melody, you may then feel it is fluent.

Alteration of Chromatic Approach

In chord progression, some voices use continuous chromatic ascending or descending to some target chord approach, hearing wise, there will be a little by little feeling of changing in the atmospheres. Generally speaking, this type of chromatic approach can be divided into two forms.

1. Within the Same Chord

If a chromatic change occurs within the same chord and only one voice part changes while others remain unchanged then this is called a "Line Cliches". This type of use appears in previous songs:

《Example II : Somewhere Over The Rainbow – Chorus》 and 《Example VI : Evergreen–Verse 1, Verse 3》 .

Also, classic songs in popular music include 「If」 of Bread, 「Kiss me」 of Sixpence None The Richer and etc., it's all right from the prelude.

Bread - 「If」

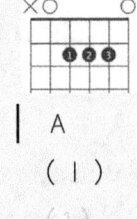

| A
(I)
(1)

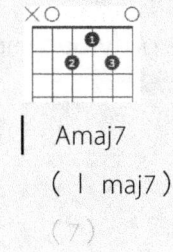

| Amaj7
(I maj7)
(7)

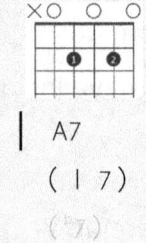

| A7
(I 7)
(7)

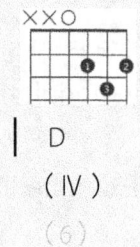

| D
(IV)
(6) |

* The above numbers represent chromatic alterations on a scale.

Sixpence None The Richer - 「Kiss me」

（Guitar capo is at the 3rd fret）

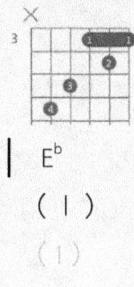

| E♭
(I)
(1)

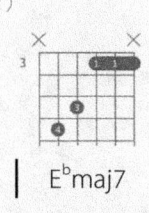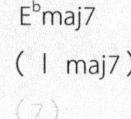

| E♭maj7
(I maj7)
(7)

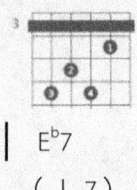

| E♭7
(I 7)
(♭7)

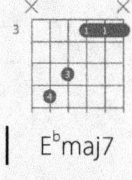

| E♭maj7
(I maj7)
(7) |

2. Different Chord Progression

　　Chromatic approach of different chord progressions often happen in the bass voice which allows this type of chromatic approach to joint with a certain chords which are not within keys, inversion chords, mixed chords or diminished seventh chords; therefore, approaches like a modal interchange and etc. are also blended inside.

There is such type of method appears in the previous repertories that follow this key modulation method have included:

《Example II : Somewhere Over The Rainbow – Verse》, 《Example V : Say Yes– Verse 2, Chorus》, 《Example VI : Evergreen– Chorus, Verse 4》 and 《Example VII : Everything》.

Also, the idea is the same for the chorus part of Bread's "If".

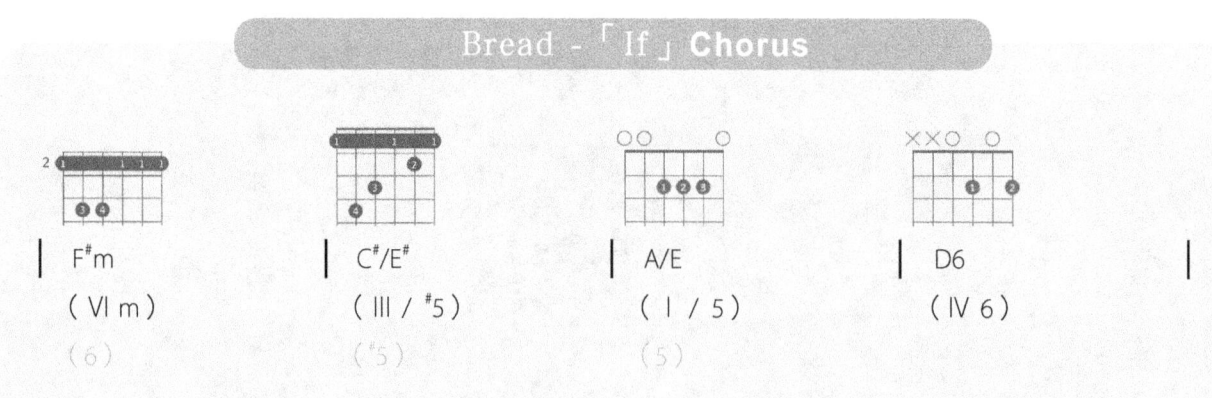

F#m	C#/E#	A/E	D6
(VI m)	(III / #5)	(I / 5)	(IV 6)
(6)	(#5)	(5)	

And identical chord progressions will also be used together with different chords and this allows the alterations of chromatic approach to be expended to a more distant chord. The entire prelude of "If" is all done with this approach.

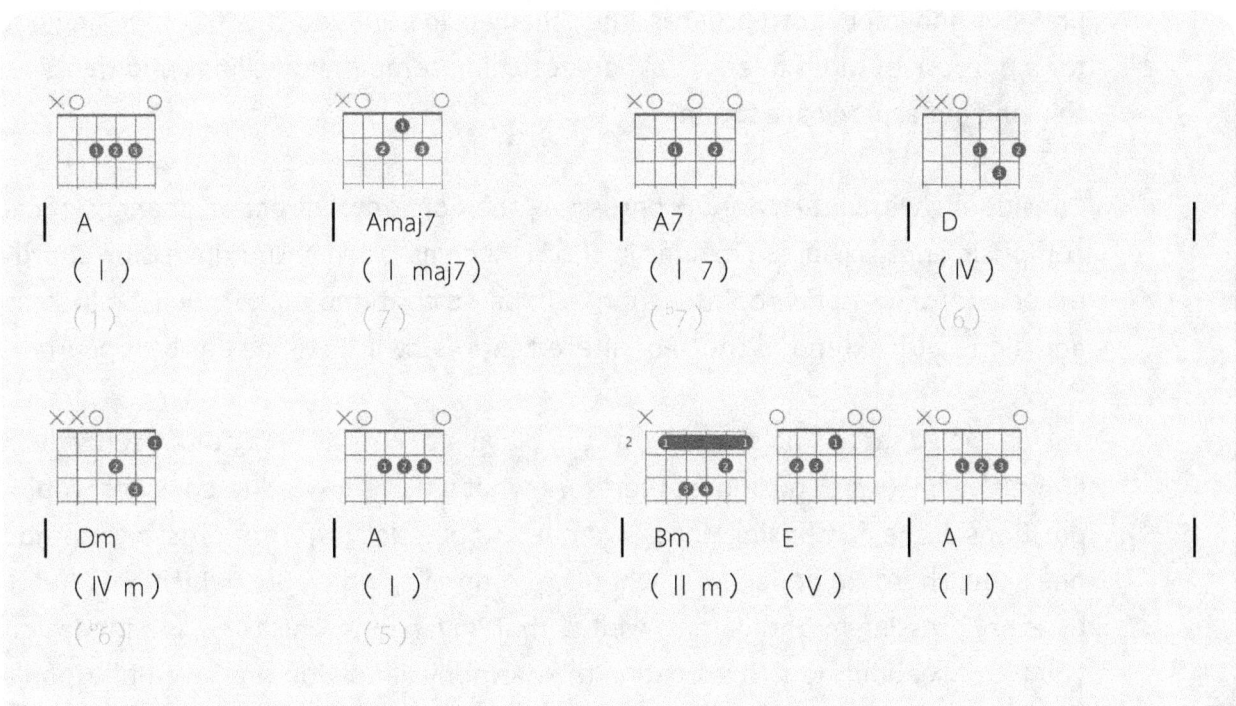

Generally speaking, this approach is often used in chords starting with I series, VI series, IV series, II series, and III series, and you can try this more often. And of course, the focus is mainly on how you feel from listening to it and not to be so limited to it. It is like the chromatic alterations 《Example V Say Yes》 which do not start from the chords above.

In addition to that, there is a temporary and precise chromatic approach with one type of Bridge or simply just a taste of passing notes. In the previous repertories, there are many areas in which passing notes are used.

Harmony Disposition

Normally when we use chords, parts that we often consider are the structure of comprising notes and atmospheres as well as feelings formed in between intervals of notes. And this belongs to more of a vertical aspect of thinking; and when we add horizontal thinking parts to our directions of thinking, for examples: it's like previous and later chord progressions, changes in between chord comprising notes for a purpose of more fluency. When designing some melodic lines and this is a thinking of harmony allocation.

Considering within the chord progression, the horizontal direction changes of chord comprising notes causes changes in chords such as, slash chord (inversion chord and mixed chord), use of chromatic approach, basso continuo and etc. will be increased and along with extended chord or altered chords, which will be easily appeared.

Taking the guitar as one example, as the playing of chords on a guitar is mostly limited by finger fret positions; therefore what we often need to consider would be positions of the comprising notes; we need to practice different pressing method of one same chord; to understand what the comprising notes are, which are affected by every pressing method are as well as their inversions. This then, is a lot easier for you to think about how to execute a the harmony allocation on the guitar upon a chord progression.

Taking a C chord as an example, there are 5 types of pressing method on a guitar:

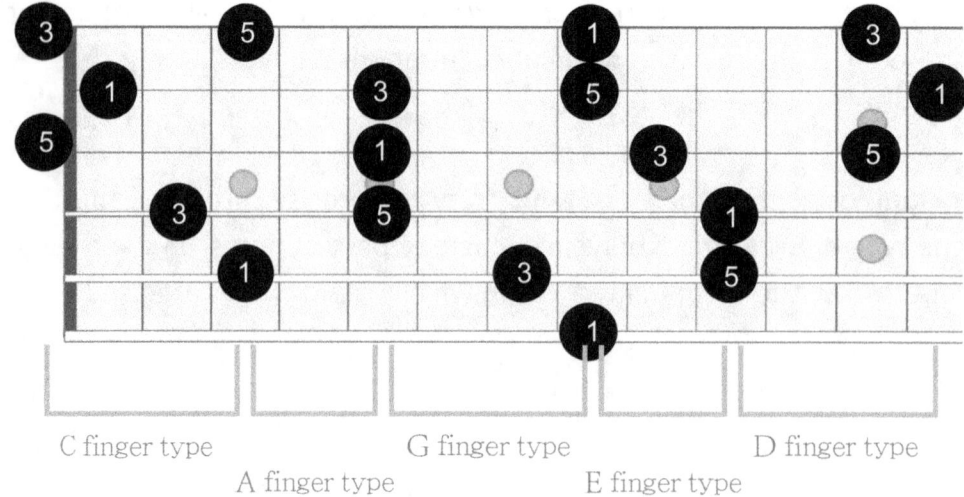

C finger type A finger type G finger type E finger type D finger type

And the root position is 1 , a 3rd note is '3' and a 5th note is '5'. We must learn to know about different pressing methods, such as which strings should be pressed specifically for the root, the 3rd and 5th notes, and we need to know what notes they belong on a scale in a certain key. It is even better that you are able to know the exact pitch names on a certain key. This way, no matter you are searching for extended notes, altered notes, or upon chord progression, it'd be relatively convenient for doing a harmony disposition; and this is so when switching to a case of inversion chord. By doing so, when changing chords on a guitar, the pressing methods would be nimble, lively and changeable, and your sense of hearing will also be more different.

For more knowledge about this type of guitar fingerboard, you can refer to another publication of mine, "Fretboard Secret Handbook". In addition to explanations, it also provides many methods on getting the familiarities and practices on fretboard notes as well as scales.

Chapter of Applications and Hands-on

After previous examples and integrated analysis，I believe you all understand these harmonic approaches. So next, please follow me and start some application exercises, allowing yourself to get used to these tools and use them naturally！

Example Ⅰ
Chord rearrangement song :

Happy Time

Original chord progression

This is a very classic Chinese folk song with the simple Four Chords. A circulation of chord progression is as below:

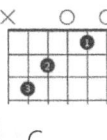   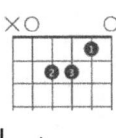   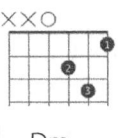   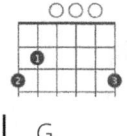

| C | Am | Dm | G |

| C | Am | Dm | G |

| C | Am | Dm | G |

| C | Am | Dm | G |

| C |

Chord rearrangement

From chord series' point of view, this is a continuous circulation of I , VI, II and V. First if we use choose an inversion chord, it would become:

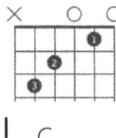   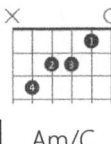   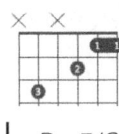   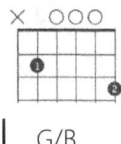

| C | Am/C | Dm7/C | G/B |

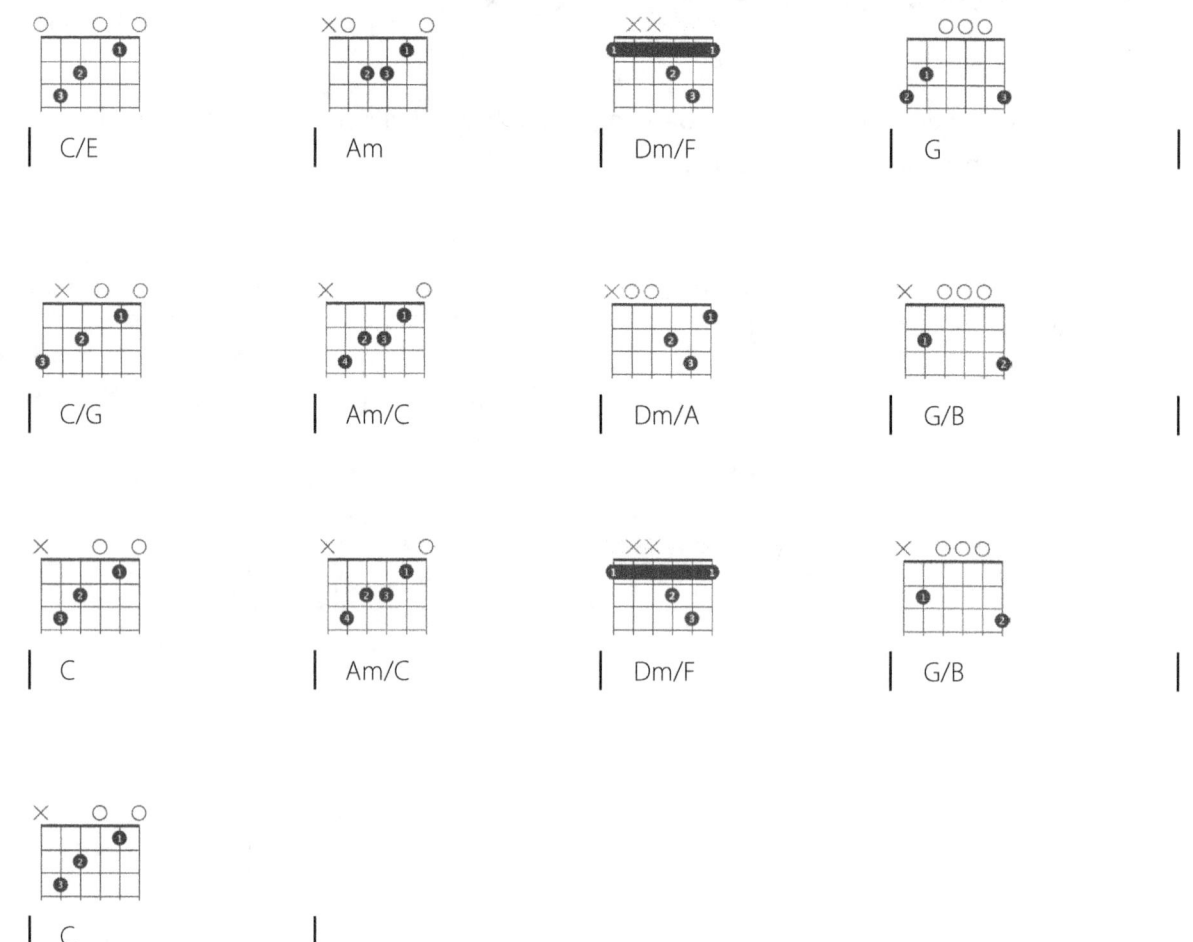

C/E	Am	Dm/F	G
C/G	Am/C	Dm/A	G/B
C	Am/C	Dm/F	G/B
C	

After making many chords into an inversion form, do they sound different?

The inversion chords I use in here has designed particularly for bass voice progressions, allowing the parallel lines of the bass voice to sound more melodically. And we can simply play the bass voice only and try feeling it.

Next let's see if we can use a modal interchange approach to change chords?

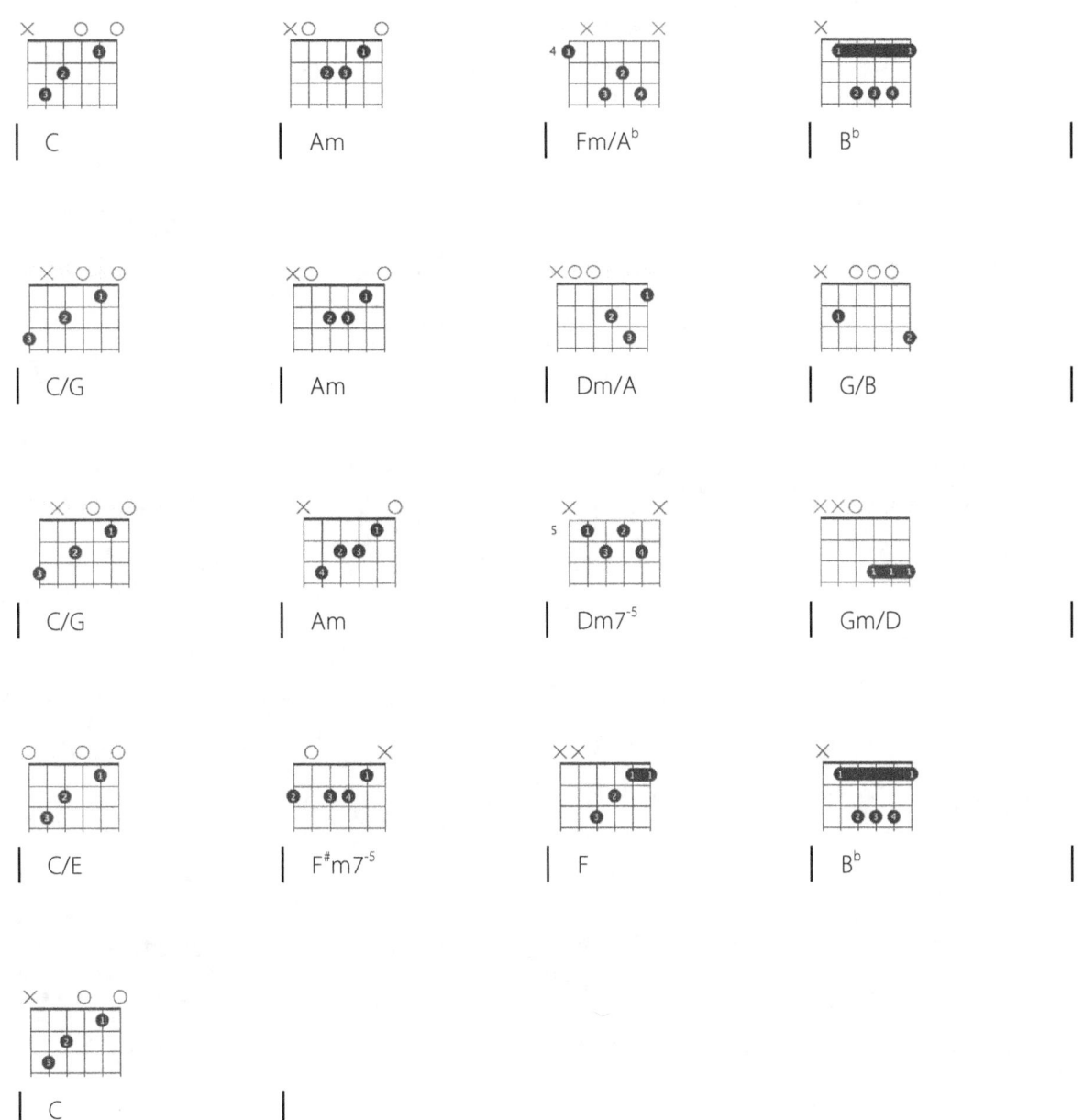

After combining with a modal interchange chord, do you feel there is more different tastes?

And of course, what you need to pay attention to is that, after changing to a modal interchange chord, you will also need to reconsider whether parallel progressions of bass voice is fluent or not in the previous and later chords. If there are parts which you don't feel to be smooth enough, then you can use inversions or other chords for adjustment; moreover, as the comprising notes after a modal interchange approach would become different, you will need to listen and see if it is unsuitable with the main melody or causes any conflicts（that is…it would sound strange, inharmonic). In here, comprising notes of Dm7⁻⁵ have a conflict with a melodic 6th note; however, you can use an accompaniment method to avoid this problem on the beat.

And next, let's try adding a diminished seventh chord, and adjust a few beat positions for the above progressions:

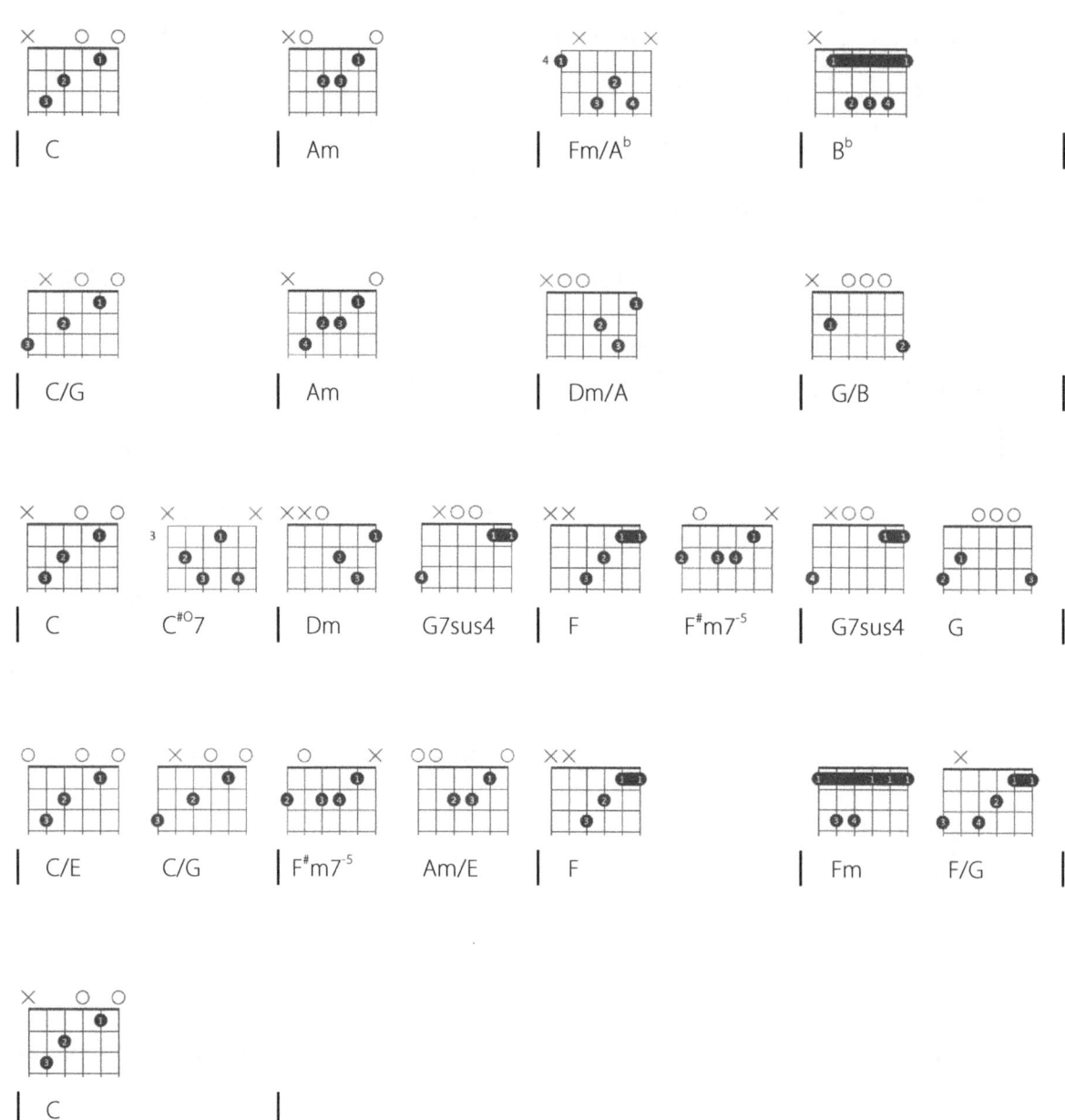

In here, I use a chromatic approach bridge method of a diminished seventh chord to allow an activation of chorus harmony and rhythm to be speeded up. Although only one chord is used, there is a more obvious distinctions for verse and chorus; and for the second chord counting from the bottom, I used a mixed chord F/G，and let's see to what place we can still add a mixed chord.

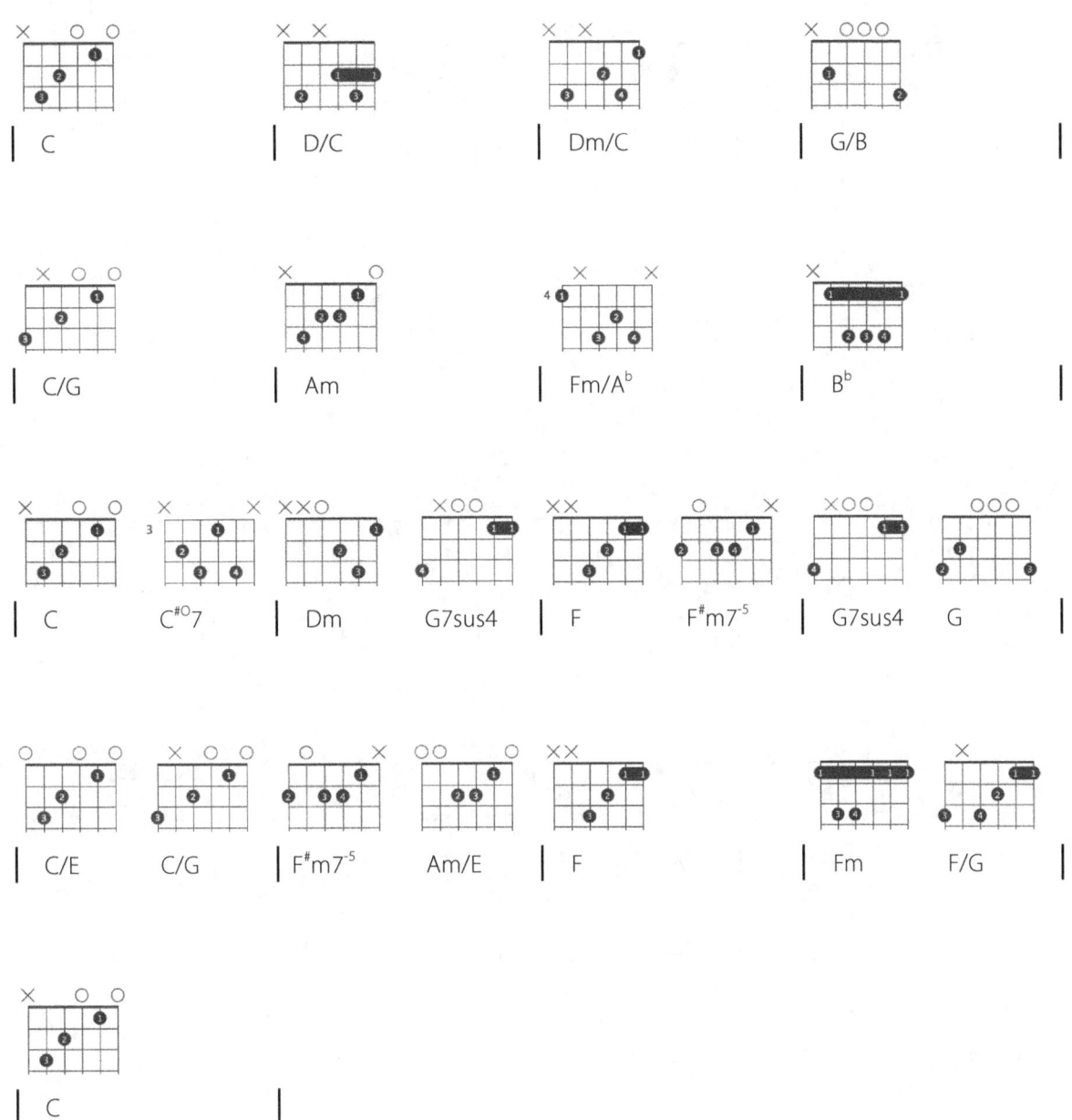

| C | D/C | Dm/C | G/B |

| C/G | Am | Fm/A♭ | B♭ |

| C C#º7 | Dm G7sus4 | F F#m7⁻⁵ | G7sus4 G |

| C/E C/G | F#m7⁻⁵ Am/E | F | Fm F/G |

| C |

First, I modified a mixed chord of Lydian modal interchange in the 2nd measure and in the later part, for a vertical direction fluency, I also changed the chords into other inversion chords. And furthermore, I switched the very smooth and good-sounding two chords which are originally in the back of the 1st line to the 2nd line and keep them there, and do no changes in the chorus.

And more, did you discover a spot that allows us to use a very special technique?

That's right, it is in the 1st line, you can see a track for using sustained notes! Let's try adding sustained notes in these chord progressions and see how the effects would be:

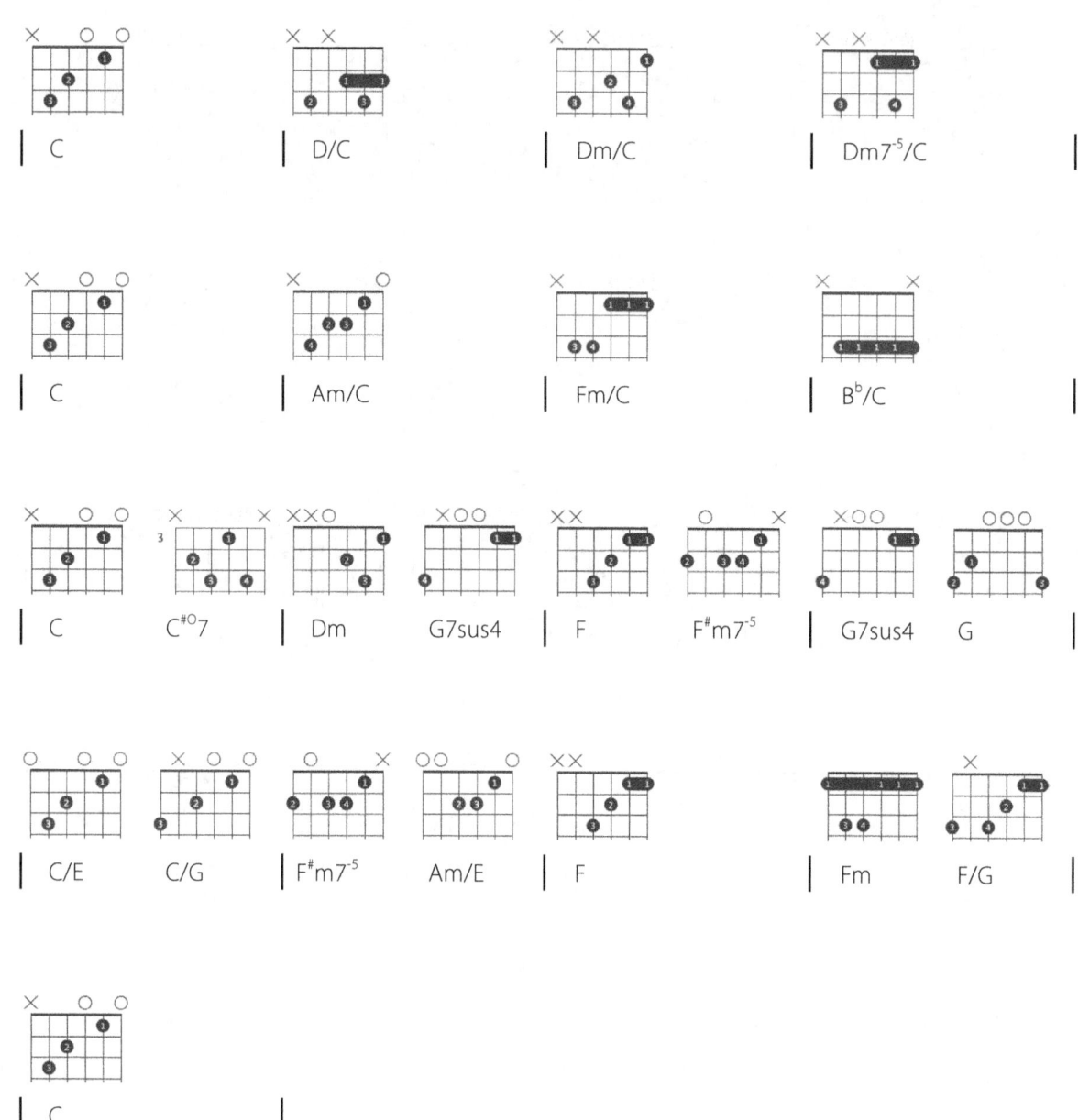

| C | D/C | Dm/C | Dm7^{-5}/C |

| C | Am/C | Fm/C | B^b/C |

| C   C$^{\#O}$7 | Dm   G7sus4 | F   F$^\#$m7^{-5} | G7sus4   G |

| C/E   C/G | F$^\#$m7^{-5} Am/E | F | Fm   F/G |

| C |

That's it, I have modified the entire Verse part into tonic sustained notes! And it is also because of such use, we have an additional mixed chord of Mixolydian （B^b/C）! The harmonic and rhythmic feelings of Verse also become very slow, isn't it quite interesting?

So far, the modifications look very much to be done, and no other approaches are needed. Unless the song is long enough with repetitions or other sections, we then can consider adding different approaches. Moreover, not all of these refining skills are needed to be used in one song. We must consider tastes, feelings and atmospheres needed by a song and then to use suitable methods.

Thus, would you say there's more room for modifications in the above section? And certainly there is.

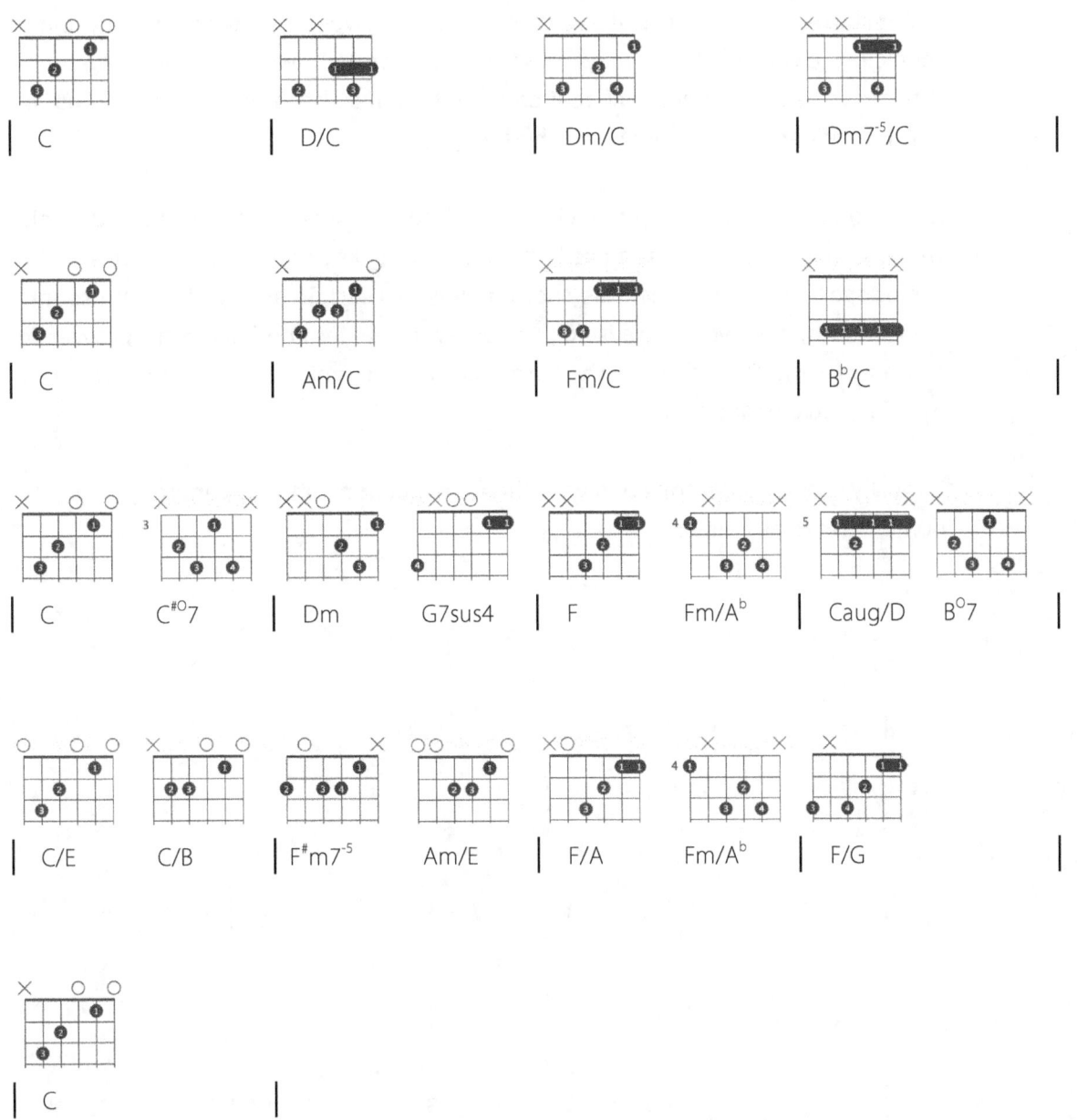

| C | D/C | Dm/C | Dm7⁻⁵/C | |

| C | Am/C | Fm/C | Bᵇ/C | |

| C   C♯°7 | Dm   G7sus4 | F   Fm/Aᵇ | Caug/D   B°7 | |

| C/E   C/B | F♯m7⁻⁵   Am/E | F/A   Fm/Aᵇ | F/G | |

| C | |

I continue to make some changes in the chorus section by adding a diminished seventh chord, mixing with altered chords and inversion chords.

Simply by doing so, you can make easy Four Chord progression to change like this, and you can also try this on your own!

For chords in some areas, if you follow a regular two-beat interval directly and then change chords, then it may not sound so smooth; however, if you move them forward to backward for a half beat count, it then may become very nice-sounding. This is a influence of harmony and rhythm.

Being on different beat position, gives us different feelings of the strong and weak. Hearing wise, there's a difference between a strong key or a 'supporting role-like'bridge. Therefore, when the chord moves to a certain area and doesn't sound very smooth; however, there is no problem with the designed harmonic progression. You may try moving a little on the harmonic position which doesn't sound to be matching on a beat position.

Basically each of the strong and weak beat on a beat position is generally demonstrated as below:

Two time：

| S | W | S | W | S | W | S | W |

Three time：

| S W W | S W W | S W W | S W W |

Four time：

| S W SS W | S W SS W | S W SS W | S W SS W |

And of course, it is not necessarily for these beats to be on beat position for a necessary result of enhancing to the hearing, in addition to this, sound volume, high or low pitches and length of a melody, the feelings of harmony itself and etc., often placing strong notes on a weak beat position for creating some effects. And also harmony and rhythm which lead to fast and slow feelings are generated due to the frequency of changing chords. For all these parts, you can try upon song writing and rearrangement on you own or to check and read theory books in details.

Example II
Chord rearrangement song：

Jingle Bell

Original chord progression

This is a very classic Christmas song, the circulation of chord progression is as below:

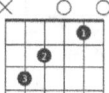
C

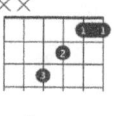
F

| 5 4 | 3 | 2 | 1 | 5 4 | — | — | — | 5 4 | 3 | 2 | 1 | 6 4 | — | — | — |

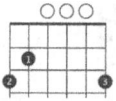
G

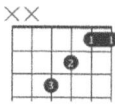
C

| 6 4 | 4 | 3 | 2 | 7 4 | — | — | — | 5 | 5 | 4 | 2 | 3 | — | — | — |

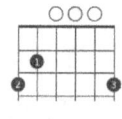
F

| 5 4 | 3 | 2 | 1 | 5 4 | — | — | — | 5 4 | 3 | 2 | 1 | 6 4 | — | — | — |

Dm   G   C

| 6 4 | 4 | 3 | 2 | 5 | 5 | 5 | 5 | 6 | 5 | 4 | 2 | 1 | — | — | — |

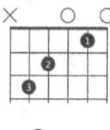
C

| 3 | 3 | 3 | — | 3 | 3 | 3 | — | 3 | 5 | 1 | 2 | 3 | — | — | — |

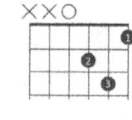
F   C   Dm   G

| 4 | 4 | 4 | 4 | 4 | 3 | 3 | 3 | 3 | 2 | 2 | 3 | 2 | — | 5 | — |

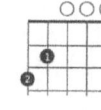

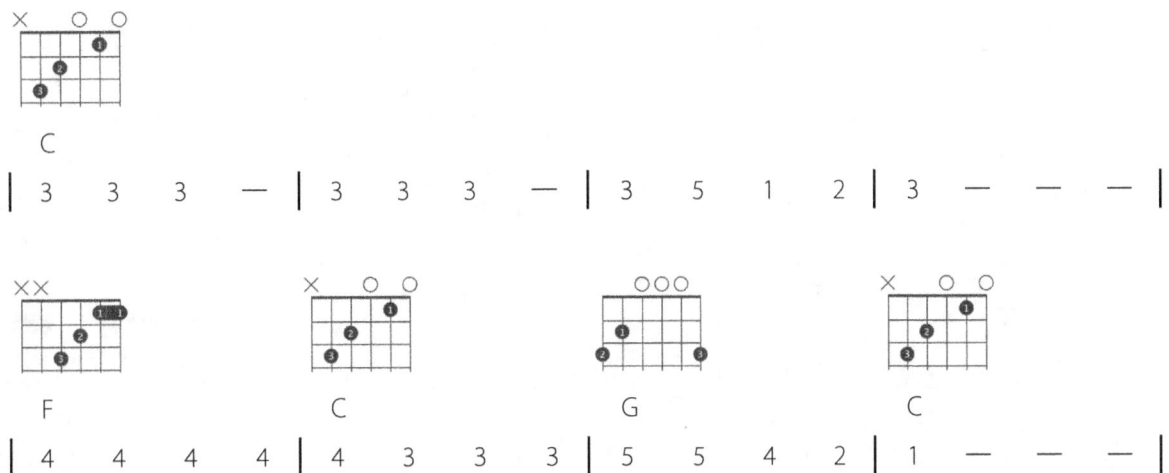

Chord rearrangement

You should be able to see chord series of this song now so we will not mention this again in here.   First of all, because I think it has fewer chords, first let us consider using a 2-5-1 method to add more chords.

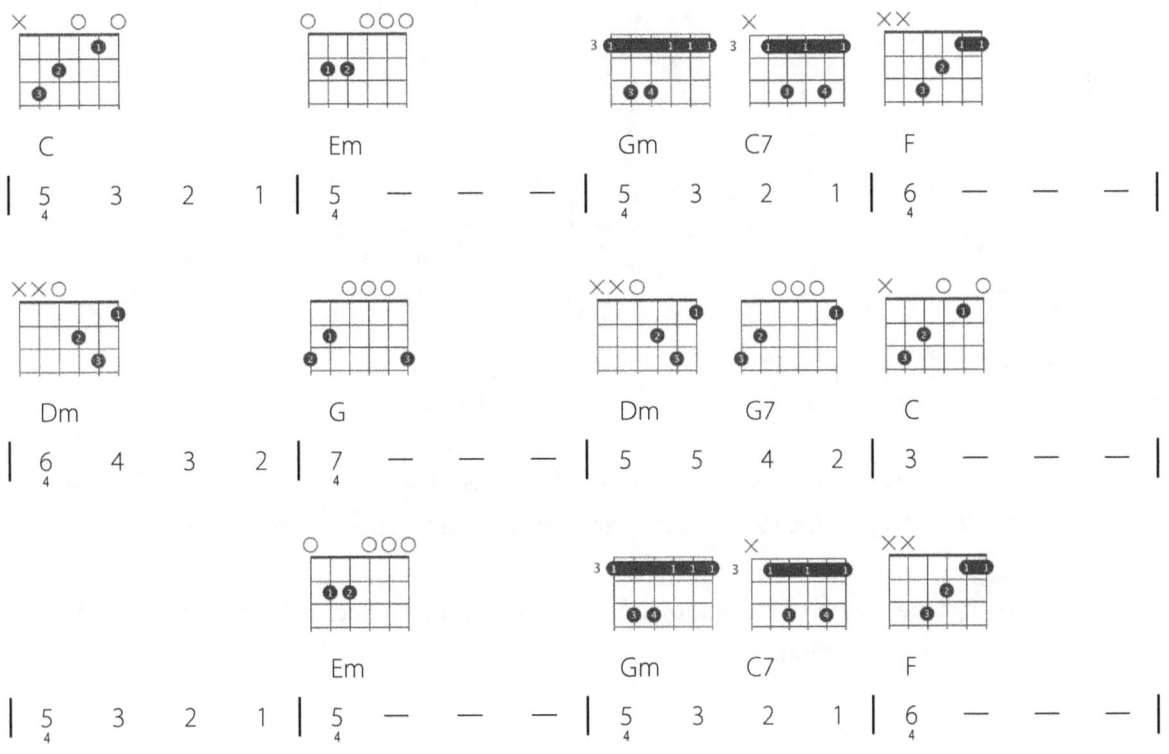

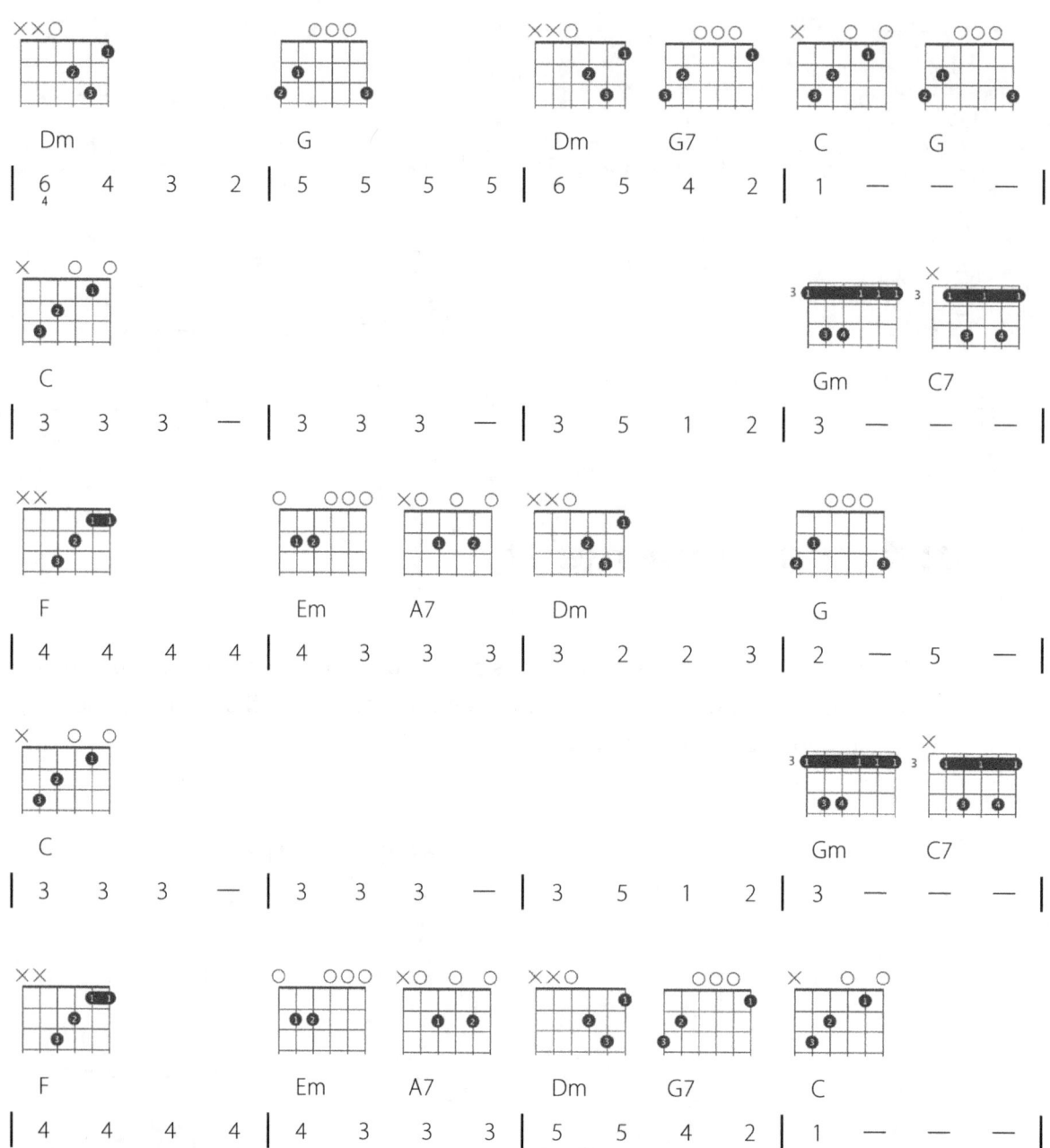

So this way we then will have quite a few more chords, don't we? The following chorus has a very lengthy C chord and is there anything else you can think of ?

Let's try Line Cliche of chromatic approach and add extra more bridge chords in the previous verse section.

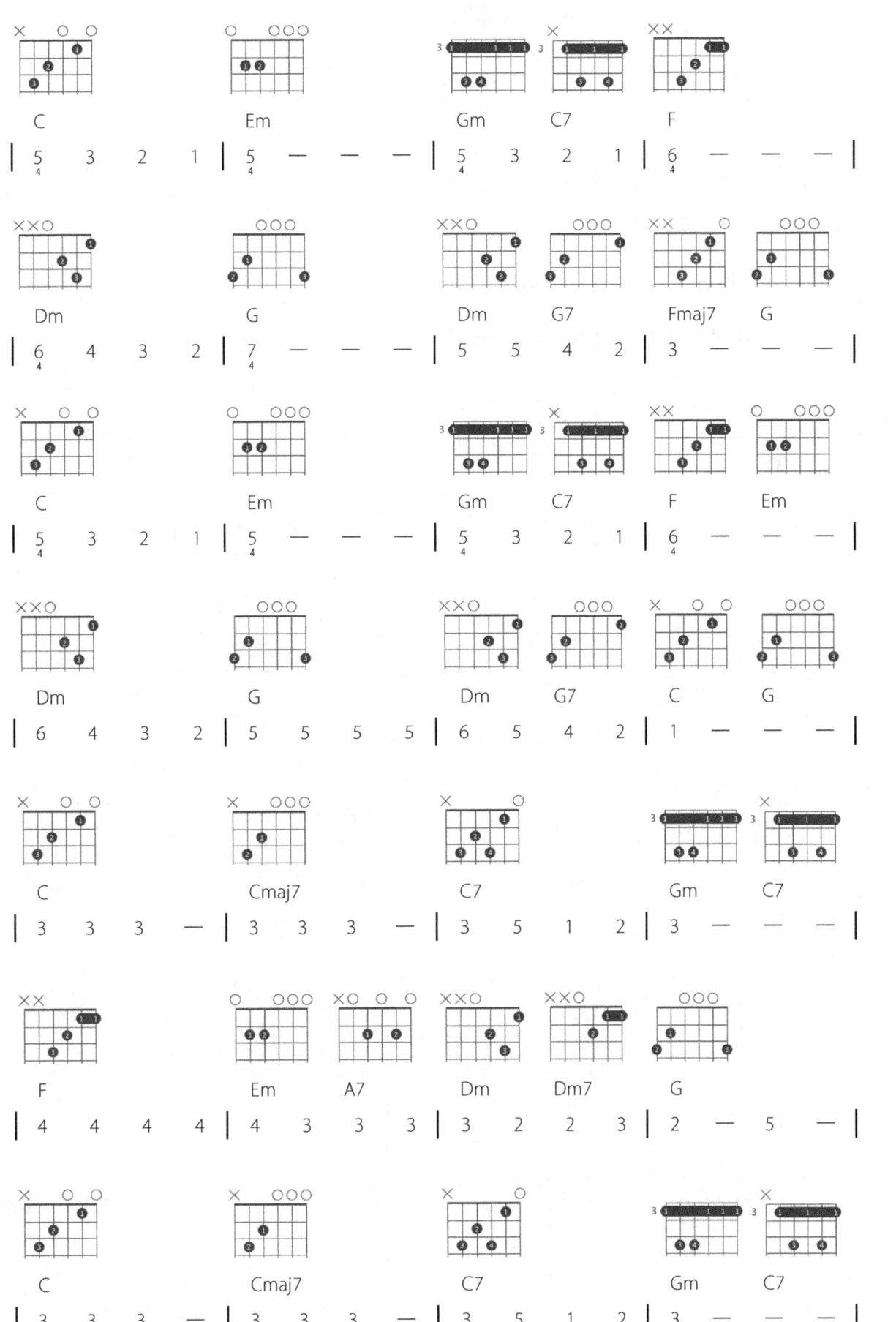

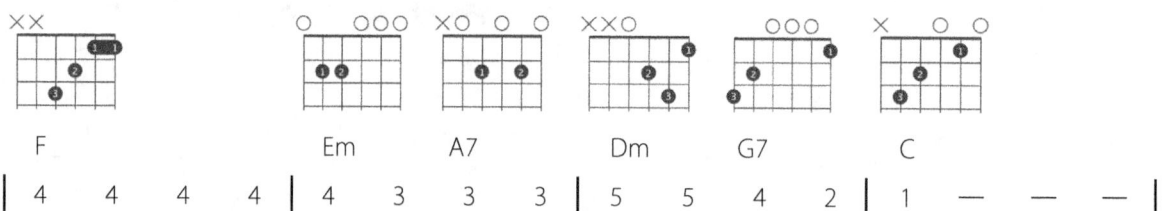

F   Em   A7   Dm   G7   C

| 4   4   4   4 | 4   3   3   3 | 5   5   4   2 | 1   —   —   — |

It looks pretty good, doesn't it ?

Shall we try a modal interchange ?

C   E♭   C   F#m7-5   F

| $\frac{5}{4}$ 3   2   1 | $\frac{5}{4}$ —   —   — | $\frac{5}{4}$ 3   2   1 | $\frac{6}{4}$ —   —   — |

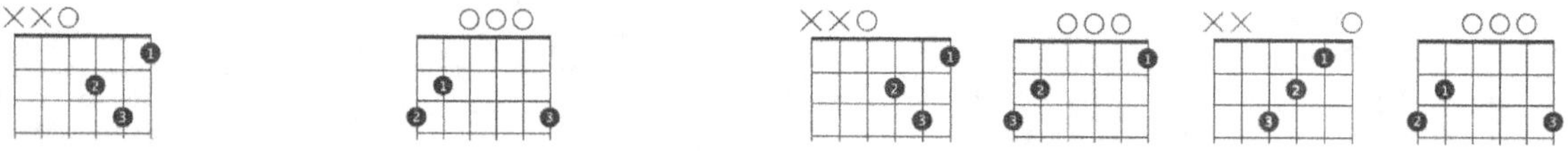

Dm   G   Dm   G7   Fmaj7   G

| $\frac{6}{4}$ 4   3   2 | $\frac{7}{4}$ —   —   — | 5   5   4   2 | 3   —   —   — |

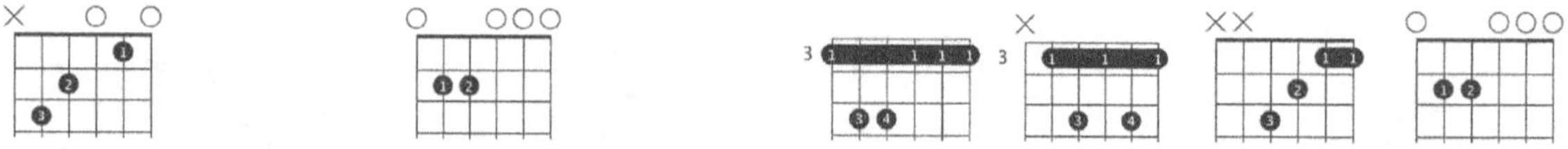

C   Em   Gm   C7   F   Em

| $\frac{5}{4}$ 3   2   1 | $\frac{5}{4}$ —   —   — | $\frac{5}{4}$ 3   2   1 | $\frac{6}{4}$ —   —   — |

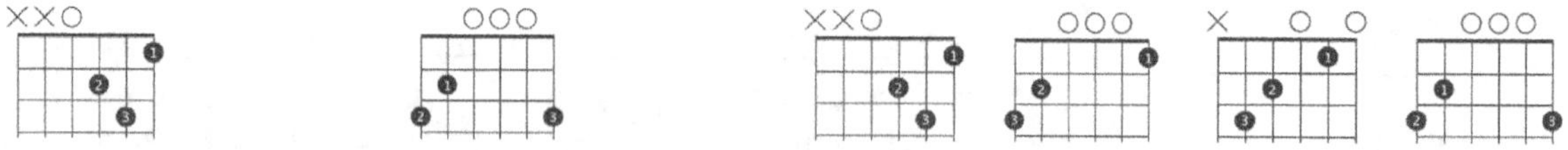

Dm   G   Dm   G7   C   G

| $\frac{6}{4}$ 4   3   2 | 5   5   5   5 | 6   5   4   2 | 1   —   —   — |

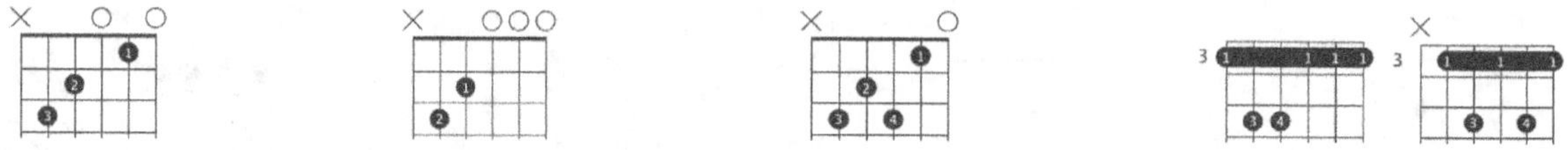

C   Cmaj7   C7   Gm   C7

| 3   3   3   — | 3   3   3   — | 3   5   1   2 | 3   —   —   — |

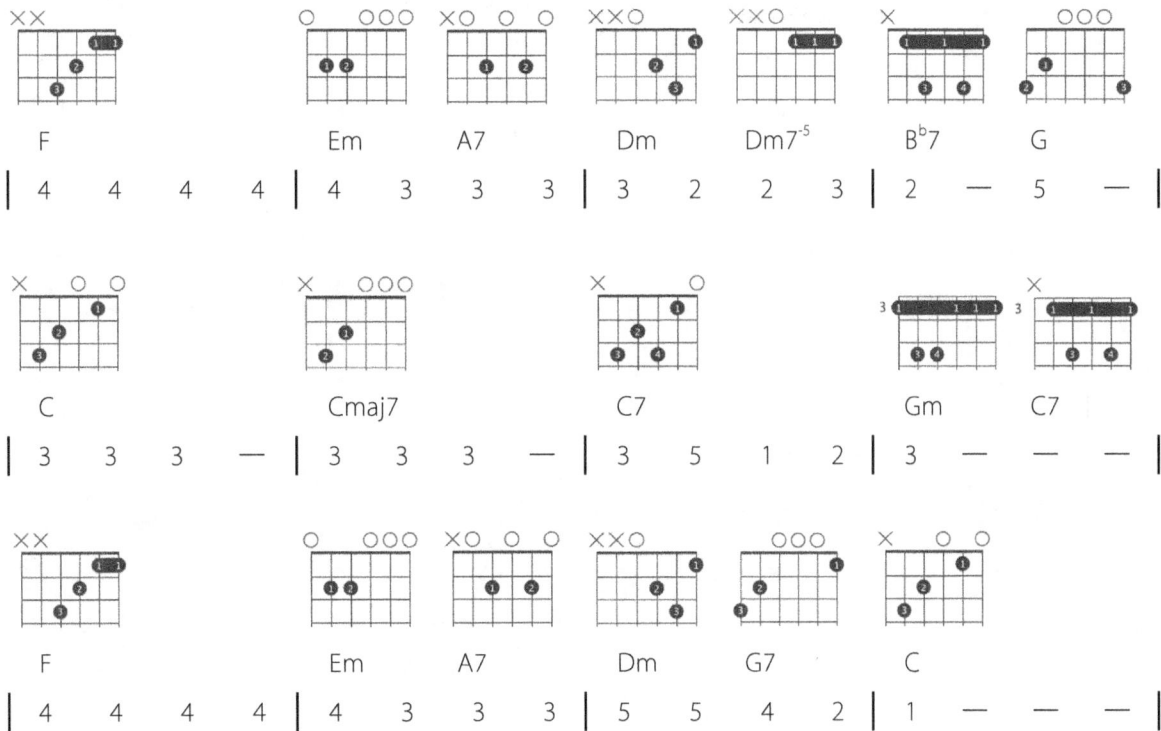

F   Em   A7   Dm   Dm7⁻⁵   B♭7   G

| 4 | 4 | 4 | 4 | 4 | 3 | 3 | 3 | 3 | 2 | 2 | 3 | 2 | — | 5 | — |

C   Cmaj7   C7   Gm   C7

| 3 | 3 | 3 | — | 3 | 3 | 3 | — | 3 | 5 | 1 | 2 | 3 | — | — | — |

F   Em   A7   Dm   G7   C

| 4 | 4 | 4 | 4 | 4 | 3 | 3 | 3 | 5 | 5 | 4 | 2 | 1 | — | — | — |

I don't use many modal interchange approaches here; instead, I mainly would like to maintain a certain structures and see what happen afterwards. Maybe after trying other approaches in the back, a modal interchange feeling will appear again in some parts.

And next, let's assume if we need to repeat for the 2nd time, is it time that we try modulating the keys? If we would like to adopt a common chord for key modulation, in the same time, we will often add an intermission section as well, allowing sufficient rooms for key modulation upon progression.

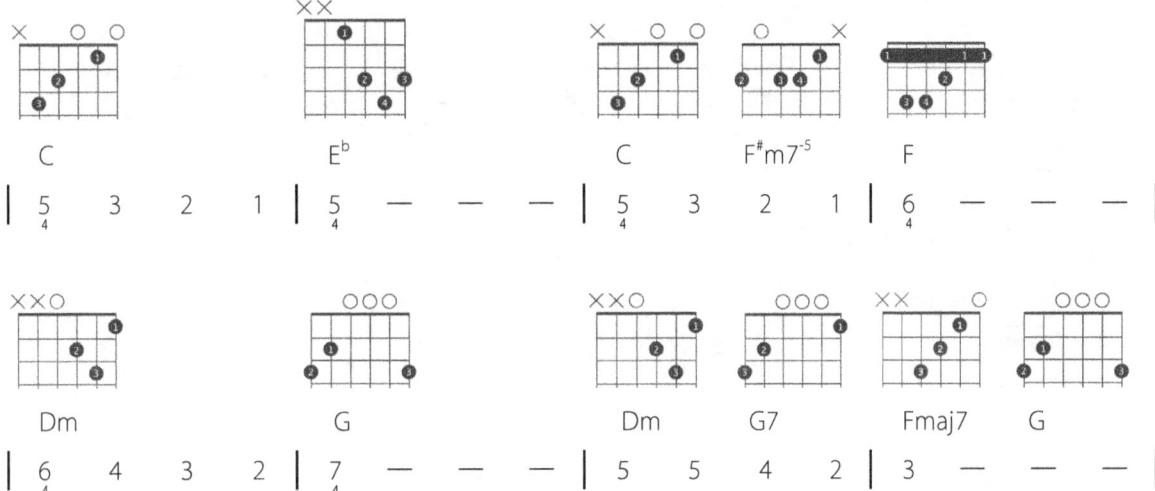

C   E♭   C   F♯m7⁻⁵   F

| 5/4 | 3 | 2 | 1 | 5/4 | — | — | — | 5/4 | 3 | 2 | 1 | 6/4 | — | — | — |

Dm   G   Dm   G7   Fmaj7   G

| 6/4 | 4 | 3 | 2 | 7/4 | — | — | — | 5 | 5 | 4 | 2 | 3 | — | — | — |

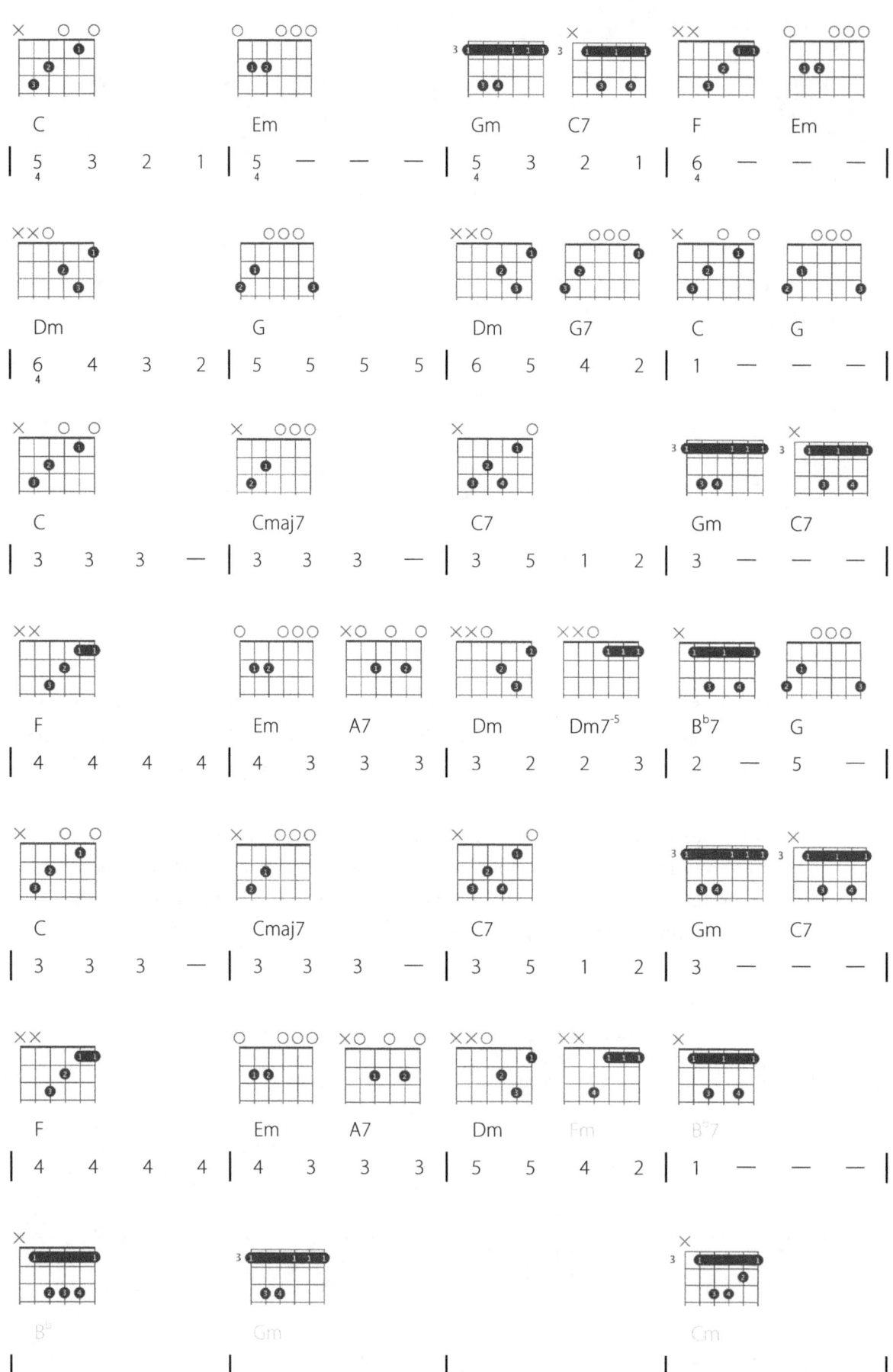

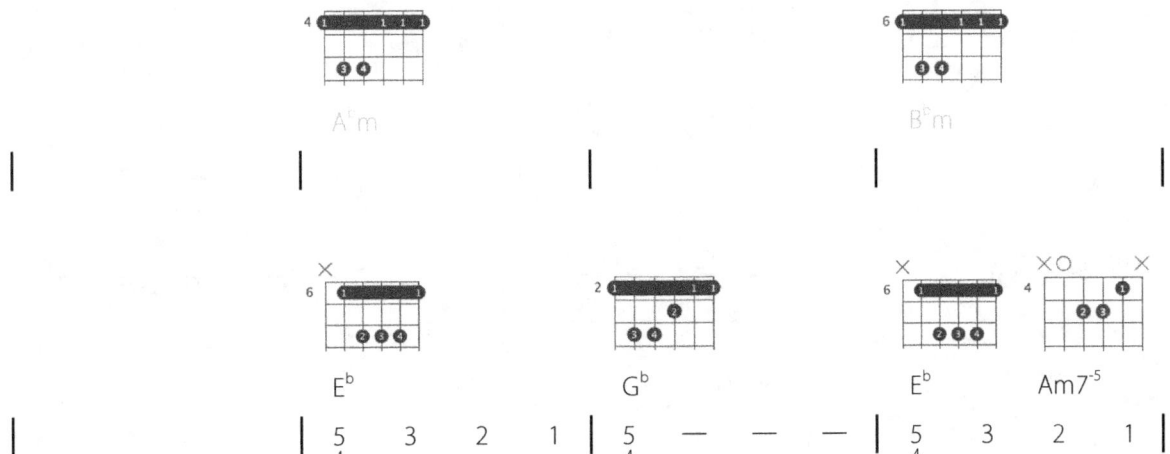

A♭m   B♭m

| | | | | |

E♭   G♭   E♭   Am7⁻⁵

| $\frac{5}{4}$ 3 2 1 | $\frac{5}{4}$ — — — | $\frac{5}{4}$ 3 2 1 |

Here it is via common chords upon a modal interchange and modulates to E♭ key. Next, let's make chord inversion a more fluent progression.

C   E♭/B♭   C/E   F♯m7⁻⁵   F

| $\frac{5}{4}$ 3 2 1 | $\frac{5}{4}$ — — — | $\frac{5}{4}$ 3 2 1 | $\frac{6}{4}$ — — — |

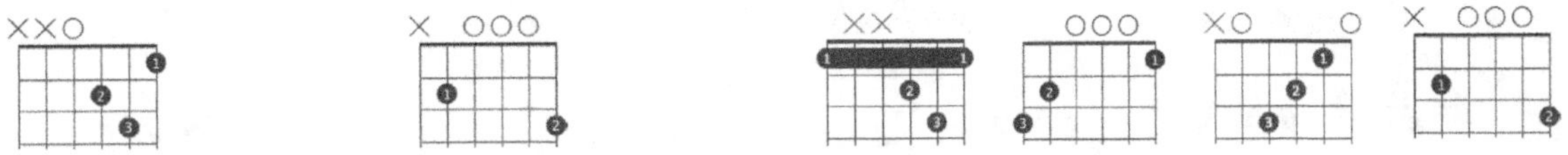

Dm   G/B   Dm/F   G7   Fmaj7/A   G/B

| $\frac{6}{4}$ 4 3 2 | $\frac{7}{4}$ — — — | 5 5 4 2 | 3 — — — |

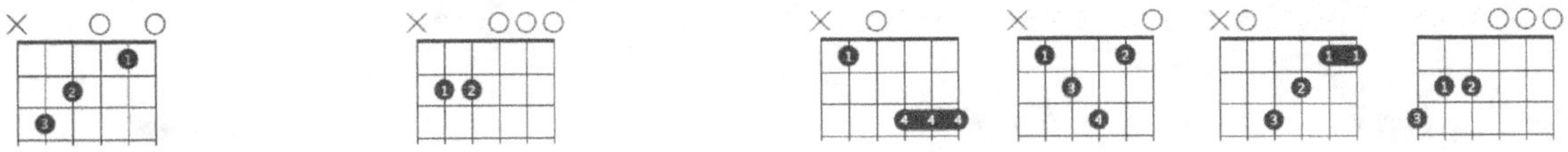

C   Em/B   Gm/B♭   C7/B♭   F/A   Em/G

| $\frac{5}{4}$ 3 2 1 | $\frac{5}{4}$ — — — | $\frac{5}{4}$ 3 2 1 | $\frac{6}{4}$ — — — |

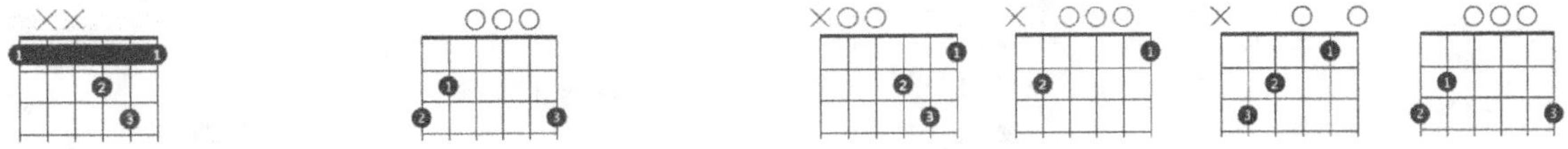

Dm/F   G   Dm/A   G7/B   C   G

| $\frac{6}{4}$ 4 3 2 | 5 5 5 5 | 6 5 4 2 | 1 — — — |

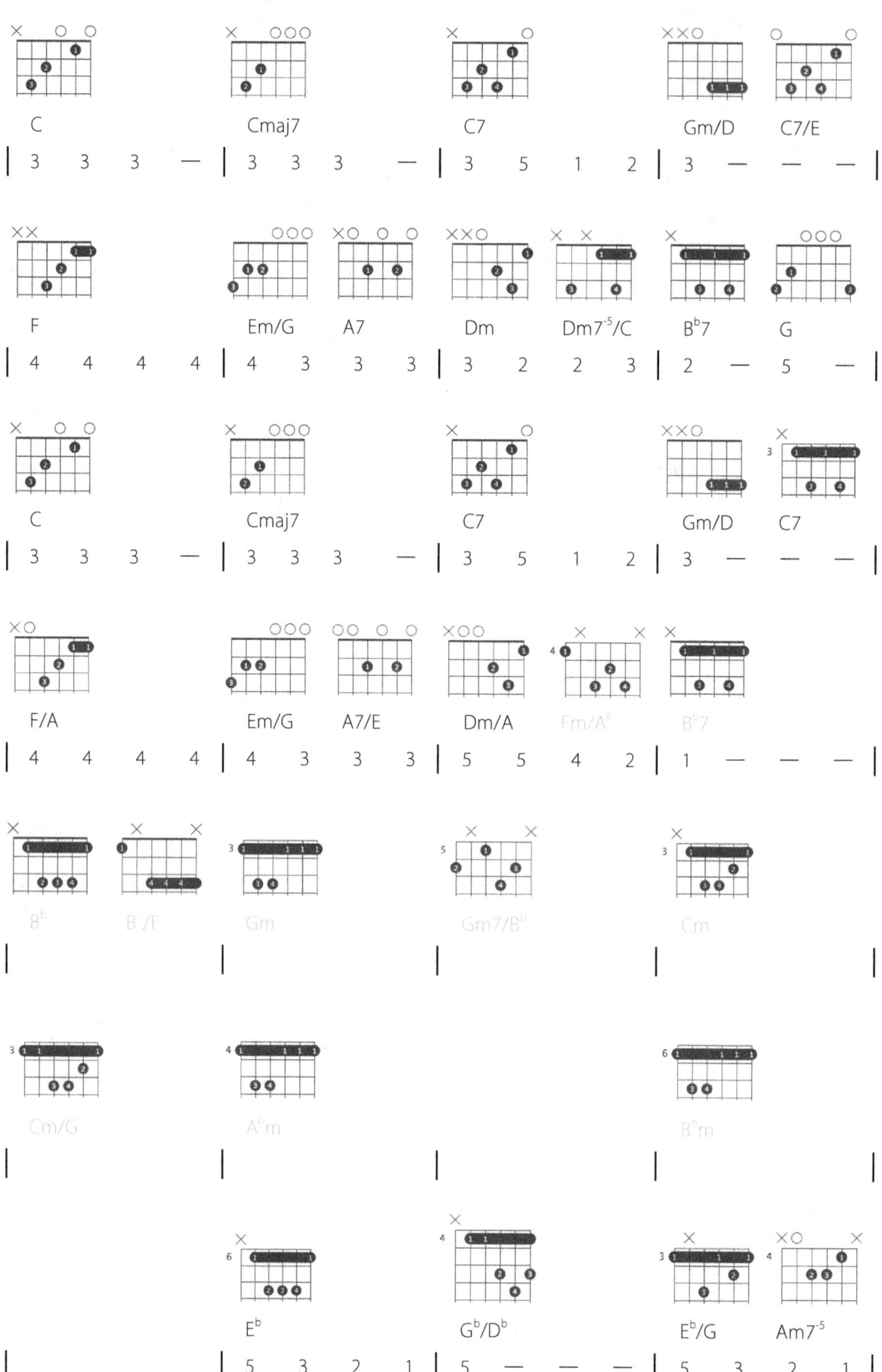

It is certainly true that after adjusting chord inversions, it sounds much better and smoother. Therefore, as you can see what an important subject an inversion is! And next, let's adjust comprising notes of a certain chords, allowing them to be better matching with the melodies.

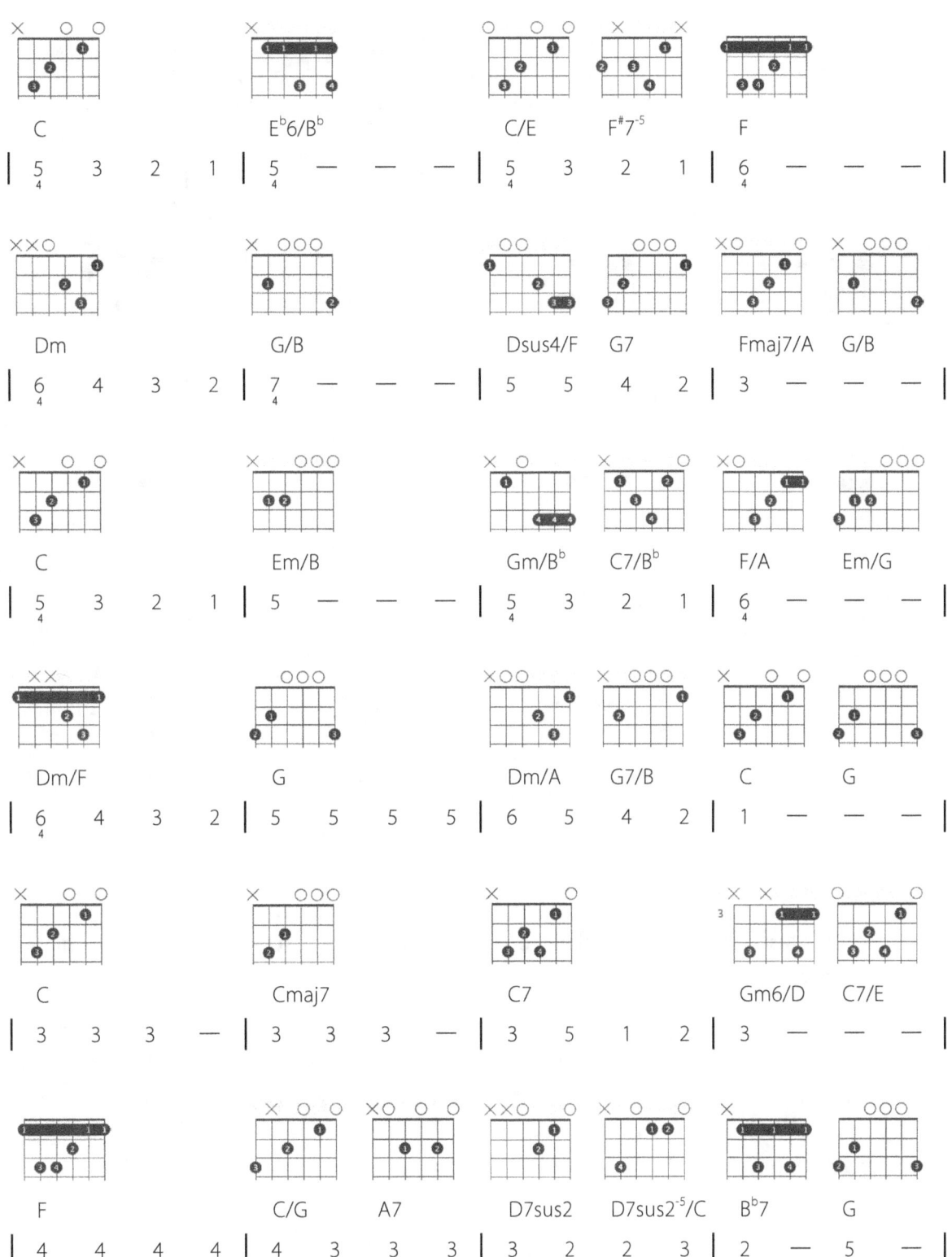

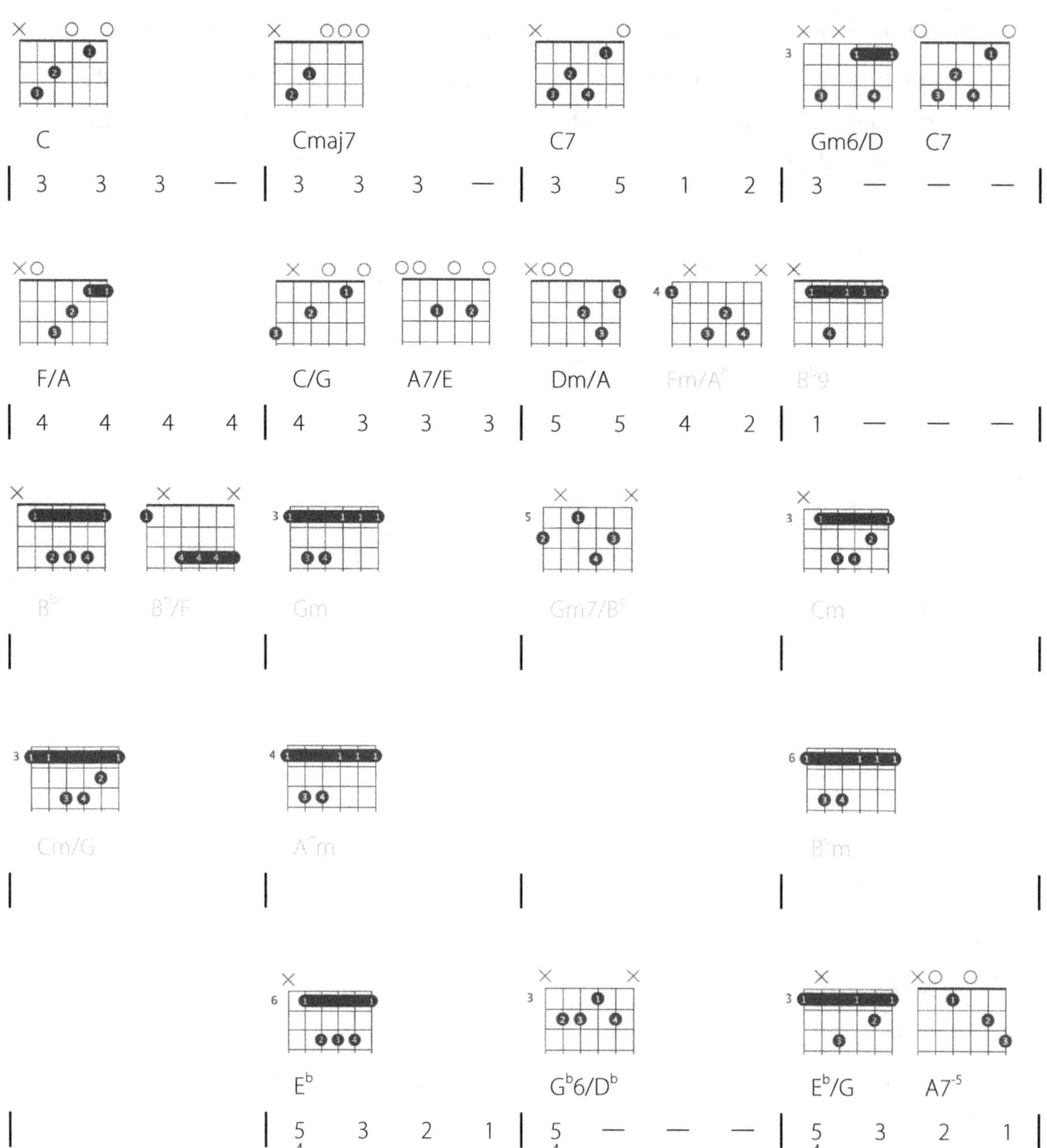

I adjust comprising notes of chords according to the pitches of melody and this way, the music sounds much smoother.

As melodies in a treble voice part are often quite distant from root, therefore when the higher notes are not a part of the original comprising notes, they then becomes a type of non-chord tones. To chords in the bottom, if we treat non-chord tone as a part of the chord, the chord then becomes a type of extended chord or altered chord, or possibly a suspended chord and etc. Therefore chord progressions which are adjusted according to melodies are often more diverse, fluent and matching.

Next let's try slightly modify dominant chords to an altered or extended chords and see:

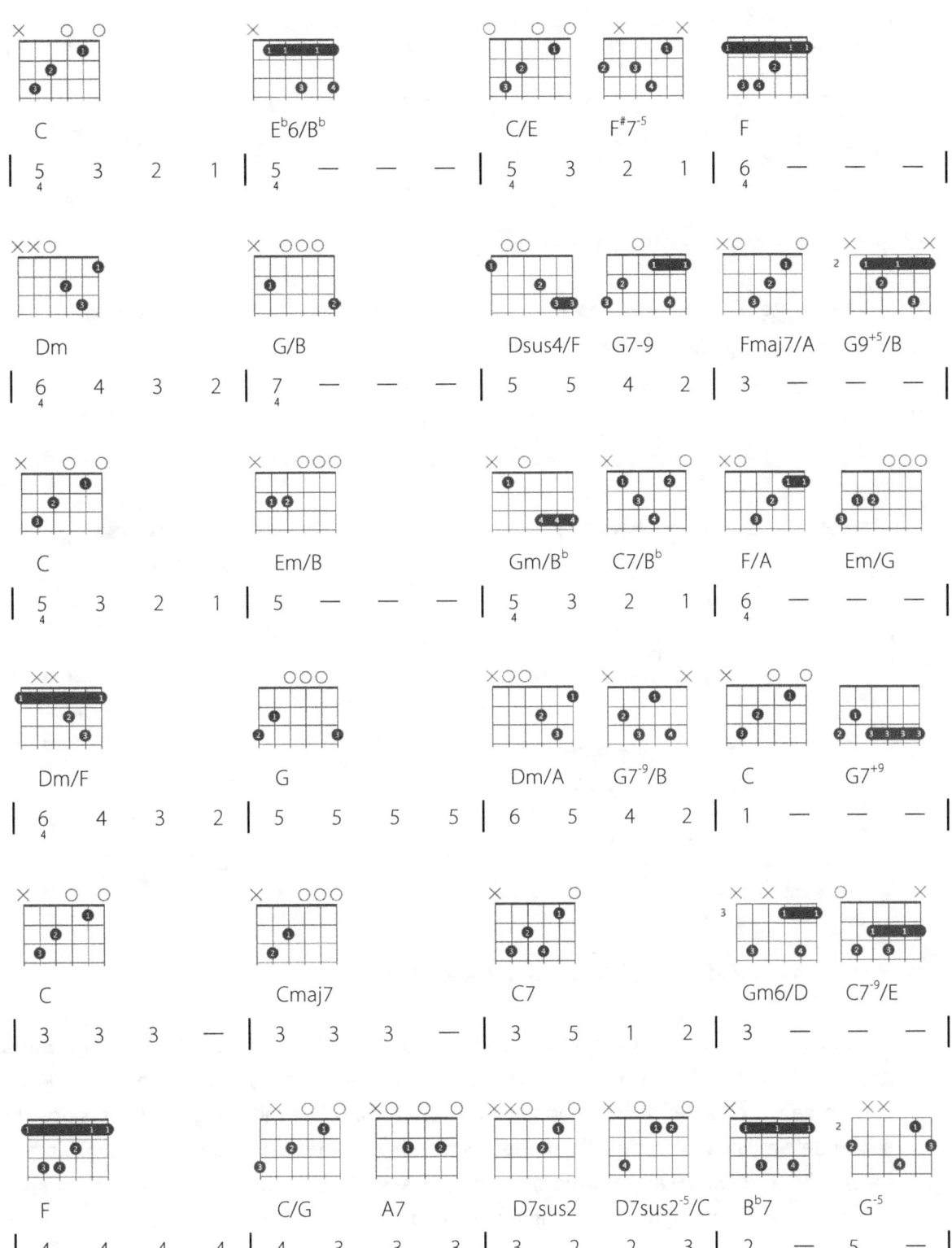

C   E♭6/B♭   C/E   F#7⁻⁵   F

| 5 | 3 | 2 | 1 | 5 | — | — | — | 5 | 3 | 2 | 1 | 6 | — | — | — |
| 4 | | | | 4 | | | | 4 | | | | 4 | | | |

Dm   G/B   Dsus4/F   G7-9   Fmaj7/A   G9⁺⁵/B

| 6 | 4 | 3 | 2 | 7 | — | — | — | 5 | 5 | 4 | 2 | 3 | — | — | — |
| 4 | | | | 4 | | | | | | | | | | | |

C   Em/B   Gm/B♭   C7/B♭   F/A   Em/G

| 5 | 3 | 2 | 1 | 5 | — | — | — | 5 | 3 | 2 | 1 | 6 | — | — | — |
| 4 | | | | | | | | 4 | | | | 4 | | | |

Dm/F   G   Dm/A   G7⁻⁹/B   C   G7⁺⁹

| 6 | 4 | 3 | 2 | 5 | 5 | 5 | 5 | 6 | 5 | 4 | 2 | 1 | — | — | — |
| 4 | | | | | | | | | | | | | | | |

C   Cmaj7   C7   Gm6/D   C7⁻⁹/E

| 3 | 3 | 3 | — | 3 | 3 | 3 | — | 3 | 5 | 1 | 2 | 3 | — | — | — |

F   C/G   A7   D7sus2   D7sus2⁻⁵/C   B♭7   G⁻⁵

| 4 | 4 | 4 | 4 | 4 | 3 | 3 | 3 | 3 | 2 | 2 | 3 | 2 | — | 5 | — |

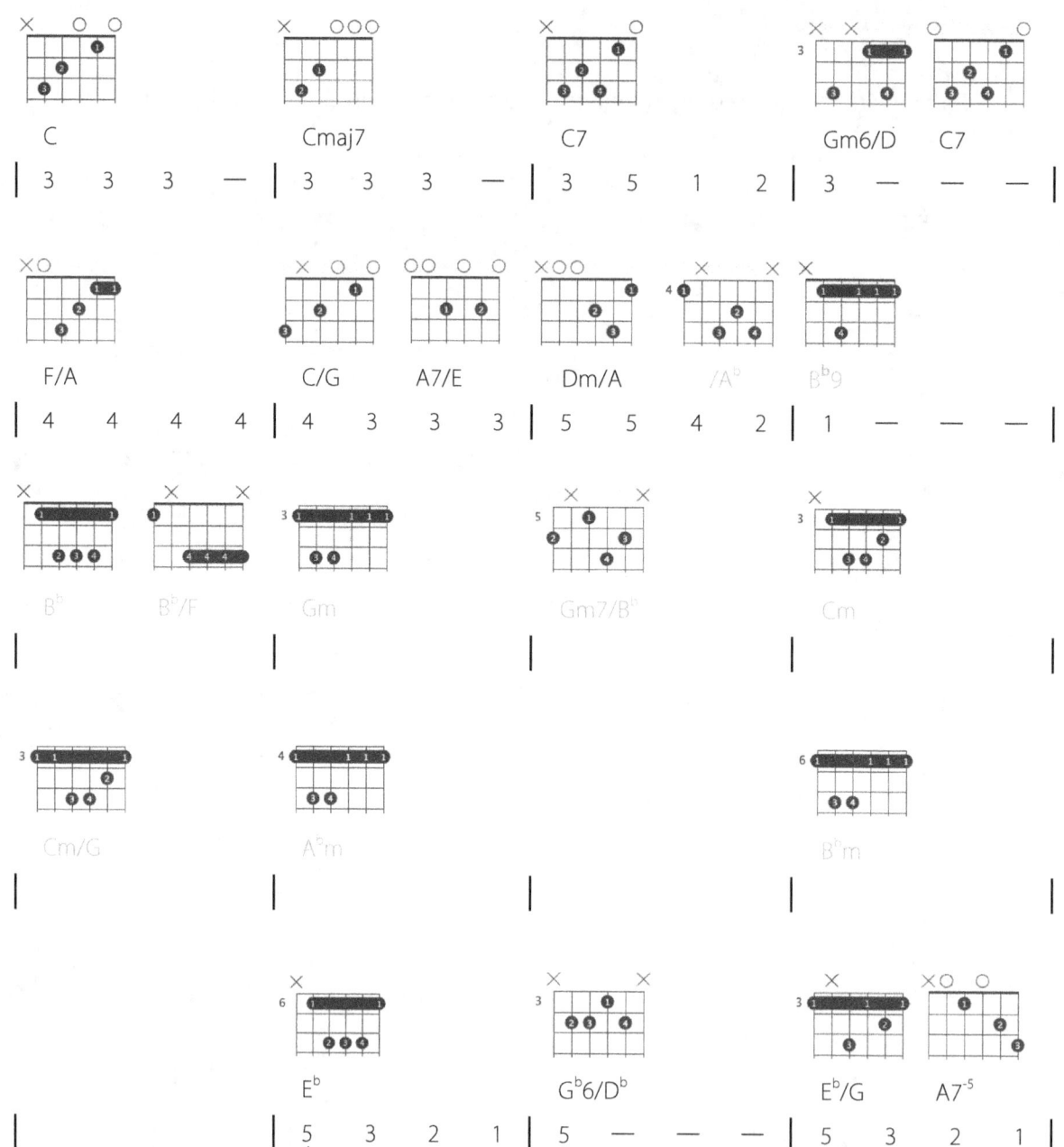

C				Cmaj7				C7				Gm6/D	C7		
3	3	3	—	3	3	3	—	3	5	1	2	3	—	—	—

F/A				C/G	A7/E	Dm/A		/A°	B♭9		
4	4	4	4	4	3	3	3	5	5	4	2	1	—	—	—

B♭   B♭/F   Gm   Gm7/B♭   Cm

Cm/G   A♭m   B♭m

E♭				G♭6/D♭				E♭/G	A7⁻⁵		

E♭	G♭6/D♭	E♭/G	A7⁻⁵
5/4 3 2 1	5/4 — — —	5/4 3 2 1

How does it sound to you? Does it sound good to you?

When we understand how to use the 'tools' of these chords, we are able to create special styles of progression that belong to us! And certainly, knowing all these approaches does not guarantee your ability to make good music. When using the same approach, it is possible that someone's music sounds stuck and not so smooth, but another person can actually make it work flawlessly. This then, will be something you can spend extra time for an experiment and study. There is no absolute right and wrong for the approaches and tools. After trying some more analysis of your favorite music, you will be able to know how other people use these approaches skillfully. And with you own experiments, you may slowly develop your own styles and special chord progressions!

Epilogue

When hearing unique harmonies, if you can try writing them down and analyze them, it will be very helpful to increase sensitivities as well as responses of your ears. When we realize how to use, listen and identify more chords, whether it is song arrangement or composition, you can absolutely be more unique at these in the long run.

And certainly, you may not be able to listen and identify as many chords as you wish in the very beginning. Therefore, at this time you can only practice via correct sheet music. When you discover new chords, please repeat your practices, feel them, and then find different pressing methods on other fret positions. And more, you would need chord practices of key transposition for the entire section and even the song. In the long run, you would feel the power of time from an accumulation of different songs; and when you hear more complicated chords upon a song search, you will also discover that you can identify types of chord and pressing method. Slowly, upon song arrangement and composition, your inspirations and thoughts will more naturally appear in your mind.

The given sample songs are not many in this book, however, there are different characteristics for each song. It would be relatively time consuming to practice until you're actually familiar with the songs. Therefore, please hold on to your very curiosity as well as a passionate heart for things that you're are familiar with, and complete the practices with patience!

Scott

Your Training Notebook on Pop Music Special Chord Progressions

Author	：Scott Su
Cover design & Interior design by	：Xinon design

"Playing Guitar So Easy"	"Fretboard Secret Handbook"
Let you easily know what easy things you can do when you play guitar at first time, and all the things that beginners want to know.	A private secret skill about memorizing the notes position and scale on guitar fretboard can really helps you to play better and better!!
Learn the basic guitar playing techniques, then easily use these methods to play songs.	This book reveals a really sufficient method for memorizing, image memory method, and combines it to the basic diatonic scale, intervals, chords, arppeggios on guitar, help many students to play freely and go further.
Start to have a wonderful musical life with your first guitar now. Play, sing and get a different happiness!!	Learn this secret skill, then you will find more about playing better with your guitar.

@ Amazon, iBook, GooglePlay, Kobo, B&N, Scribd.... and more.